Affirmative Parenting

By

Dale S. Sheffield, Ph.D.

Copyright © 2019 Dale Sheffield
All rights reserved

No part of this book may be reproduced in any form or by any electronic or mechanical means including information storage and retrieval systems, without permission in writing from the author. The only exception is by a reviewer, who may quote short excerpts in a published review.

The information presented herein represents the views of the author as of the date of publication. This book is presented for informational purposes only. Due to the rate at which conditions change, the author reserves the right to alter and update his opinions at any time. While every attempt has been made to verify the information in this book, the author does not assume any responsibility for errors, inaccuracies, or omissions.

This book is not intended as a substitute for the medical advice of physicians. The reader should regularly consult a physician in matters relating to mental or physical health and particularly with respect to any symptoms that may require diagnosis or medical attention.

Contents

Preface 1
Introduction 4
Chapter 1: The Shaping of a Child 7
    Your Body, Brain, and Hormones 9
    Adverse Childhood Experiences (ACEs) 13
    Stress and Gene Expression 15
Chapter 2: Creating an Autonomous Environment ... 20
    We Are Not Puppets of the Universe 21
    Developing Autonomy 23
    This Does Not Mean Let Your Child Run Wild 26
        The Bare Minimum 27
Chapter 3: Balancing Safety and Freedom 30
    Physical Safety—Baby 31
    Physical Safety—Childhood 34
    Gun Safety 35
    "Stranger Danger": Use Facts, Not Fear 38
    Don't Keep Your Child Isolated 41
    Food Safety 43
Chapter 4: Healthy Parental Responses 46
    The Parents' Response Provides a Lesson 48
    When Your Child Crosses the Line, First Get the Facts ... 50
    Keep Your Eye on the Goal 52
    We All Make Mistakes 53

Children Model Their Parents 54
Chapter 5: Discipline 58
    Corporal Punishment at Home 63
    The Way Forward 64
    Toddlers and Young Children: A Reality Check 69
Chapter 6: Attachment and Exploration 72
    Ainsworth's "Strange Situation" 74
        1. Secure 75
        2. Anxious-avoidant, insecure 76
        3. Anxious-ambivalent/resistant, insecure 77
        4. Disorganized/disoriented 78
    Reactive Attachment Disorder (RAD) 79
    Piaget and the Importance of Exploration 81
        1. Sensorimotor stage: birth to two years 82
        2. Preoperational stage: ages two to seven 83
        3. Concrete operational stage: ages seven to eleven 84
        4. Formal operational stage: ages twelve and up 85
    Play Is Exploration 86
Chapter 7: Empathy 89
    Bullying 96
    Stages and Steps 98
        Age Zero to Two 98
        Three and Four 100
        Five and Six 101

Empathy, a Non-Cognitive Prosocial Skill, Should Be Learned Early 102
Chapter 8: Daycare and the Myth of Socialization 105
The Great Daycare Debate 108
Socialization 110
The Strong Parental Bond 113
John Bowlby's Attachment Theory 114
The 44 Thieves Study 116
Do the Best You Can 117
Chapter 9: Potty Training 121
When Do We Start? 123
Chapter 10: Temper Tantrums 127
Behavioral Disorders 131
Chapter 11: Morality and Conscience 135
The Lying Time Line 136
Teenage Lying 143
Cults 145
Chapter 12: Eating Disorders 149
Psychological Diseases That Affect Children 152
Obsessive-Compulsive Disorder (OCD) 152
Eating Disorders 153
Nonsuicidal Self-Injury (NSSI) 153
The Affirmative Parenting Response 155
1. Watch, Ask, and Listen 155
2. Do Not Blame Yourself 156

3. Get Informed	156
4. Visit Your Pediatrician	159
5. Find an Eating Disorders Specialist	159
6. Be Careful with Drugs	160
7. Seek Support for Yourself	162
Chapter 13: Tiger Mom, Elephant Mom, Helicopter Parent	163
The Four Parenting Styles	168
1. Authoritarian	168
2. Authoritative	169
3. Permissive	169
4. Neglectful	170
The Affirmative Parent	171
Chapter 14: The Truth About the Child's Biological Parent	173
Thank You	179
About the Author	180
Publications	181
Acknowledgements	182

Preface

When I was growing up, I found myself on the receiving end of powerful negative behaviors and communications from my parents. At the time, this abuse seemed "normal," but later I realized it had caused emotional problems including deep-seated insecurity. I believe my parents were essentially good people, and they did not intentionally cause me harm. In fact, there were many times during my childhood when they expressed compassion, empathy, and love. However, too often their frustration and anger consumed them, resulting in harsh physical or emotional punishments. Even worse, they both could dole out unrelenting verbal criticism that was soul-crushing. My dad was particularly skilled in this area. My mom could be as well but to a lesser degree.

Fortunately, instead of engaging in self-harm, as many young adults do, at the age of twenty-four I sought psychotherapy, which was helpful and lasted several years.

As I write this, my parents are both deceased. My dad died in 1995 and my mom passed in 1998. At the time of his death, the relationship between my dad and me was good, and probably the healthiest it had ever been. The same was true for my mom and me. I mention this only to demonstrate there's always hope, and even if you are estranged from your parents, or from your children, the passage of time and open hearts can often bring people together.

On the other hand, in some families, it's just as well that parents and adult children never speak to each other. You see this in families where either the parent or the child exists in a realm that's just too far removed from an affirmative place to make a rapprochement possible. I've known people who have said to me, "It would have been better if my father/mother had died when I was a kid. At least then I could have created some happy memories. But now my father/mother is seventy years old and still as nasty as ever. We haven't spoken in ten years, and I don't plan on speaking to them for the next ten years. When I try, they always say something mean, and we get into a fight. I'm not going to allow that to happen again."

Perhaps it was my intensely stressful experience as a child that motivated me to become a psychotherapist, with a mission to help young parents interact with their children in an emotionally and psychologically affirmative manner. Over the years, I came to understand that it's never too early to start, and in fact, parents should learn before their children are born the healthy approaches to child-rearing from birth through the early twenties and beyond. The phrase, "An ounce of prevention is worth a pound of cure" is exponentially true with regards to parenting. It is much more difficult to help a child after his or her emotional growth has been impaired or stunted due to poor parenting versus helping a child stay healthy by achieving emotional developmental milestones provided by affirmative parenting. In other words, it is easier to move forward into the future if you do not have to go back and repair the past.

The phrase, "Sticks and stones can break my bones, but words can never hurt me" is untrue! The words of my parents hurt me plenty, resulting in a child with severely low self-esteem, problems with anger, anxiety issues, and depression. As I stated, they did not intentionally set out to cause me these problems but that was the result.

With my practice as a psychotherapist supplemented by this book, my goal is to help parents raise children who are self-confident, empathic, and loving people.

Introduction

Welcome to *Affirmative Parenting*.

The goal of this book is to provide you with a road map to raising a child who will grow up to be happy, loving, self-sufficient, and engaged in life.

Raising children is a complicated business. Especially for the first-time parent, childrearing is full of new experiences, rules to learn, decisions to make, and dangers to avoid. Sometimes the job is made easier by responsible grandparents or other caregivers who can lend support and advice, and sometimes the job is made more difficult by those same well-meaning people who seem to have an answer for everything and don't hesitate to let you know what you're doing wrong.

The goal of this book is to make your job easier and more enjoyable. It's not intended to intimidate you with endless theories and dire warnings about all the things that could go wrong between birth and your child's entrance into adulthood. It's designed to provide a positive set of directions, which I think you'll agree, are based on simple common sense.

The book begins with an overview of the beautiful and breathtaking complexity of the human body, and how the infant brain and its functions are shaped by both genetics and childhood experiences. As a parent, you can't change the former, but you have a lot of influence over the latter.

Creating an autonomous environment is important, which means providing space for your child to make some of their own decisions while keeping clear boundaries. It's your job to balance safety and freedom so that your child has the opportunity to explore both physically and creatively while always having a safe "home base" to return to.

How you respond to your child is important. All children make mistakes, and all children can be vexing. Your child will test you to see your reaction to pushing the limits. If you tell your child to never put the teddy bear in the toilet, you can be sure that soon thereafter your child will, in full view of you, dangle the teddy bear over the toilet while looking you in the eye. This is a test to see how you'll respond, and with the help of this book, you'll handle the situation with grace and good spirits.

Every child needs discipline, but you need to approach it in a positive, affirmative way by focusing on what the child should do rather than on what the child *shouldn't* do. You'll discover that it's a lot more effective to say, "Yes, do this!" rather than, "No, don't do that."

Bullying has become a problem among young people, and it's important to know that bullies come from a place of insecurity. If your child shows signs of being a bully, it probably arises from a sense of anger and alienation, and as the affirmative parent, you can do a lot to bolster your child's sense of self-confidence as well as their empathy.

Lying, eating disorders, self-injury, and other difficult behaviors may arise, and with this book you'll be equipped to take steps to identify them, connect with your child, and if necessary, seek professional assistance.

It's also important to occasionally take a look in the mirror. Are you a tiger mom (or dad)? Or maybe a helicopter parent? Sometimes we love our kids so much that we go overboard and try to either direct or protect them too much.

The goal is to raise a child who will grow up to be happy, loving, self-sufficient, and engaged in life. With the help of this book, as long as you keep aiming at that destination, you—and your child—will do very well.

Ready? Let's get started.

Chapter 1: The Shaping of a Child

Imagine you have been dropped onto a strange planet. None of its features are familiar to you. You feel tiny and defenseless, and at the mercy of your environment. You soon discover you have a place to live, which you share with larger, more powerful beings who look like you, only much lumpier and hairier. These big people can do lots of things you cannot do, chief among them being the preparing and presenting of food. In fact, you quickly learn that unless these big people give you food, you'd starve. But sometimes the reverse is true, and the big people seem determined to shove more food down your throat than you could ever eat. It's very confusing.

The big people also have physical control over your actions—for example, they can pick you up, and then either protect you and comfort you or inflict pain. Being comforted is a good thing. Receiving abuse is a bad thing, and what can make it even more painful is that sometimes you have no idea why the big people are angry at you. Most horrifying of all, there are times when the big people, or a particular big person, inflict pain on you for no other reason than you exist.

They attack you simply because you're there—but you didn't ask to be there. You fell from the sky and woke up, and there you are, living in a house with these big, powerful, and unpredictable people.

You do your best to appease them and elicit from them love rather than pain. You quickly learn that to get along, you go along. This means you emulate what they do. If the big person beats the dog, then beating the dog must a good thing to do. If the big person beats you, then beating other, smaller creatures must be what they want you to do.

Aside from the immediate question of your safety and emotional comfort, how the big people treat you is extremely important for two reasons.

The first reason is that as you grow, you're learning about the world and how to survive in it. The examples set by the big people—and then later on by your peers, who are also learning—serve as your road map. What is done to you will be reflected in how you treat others. How could it be otherwise? If they teach you the best way to survive is to be fearful, then it's likely you'll grow up to be fearful and averse to risk. If they teach you that people of a different race or religion are bad, then that's what you'll believe. If they teach you that girls can't do math or science, then who are you to think differently?

The second reason is that you are growing and developing, both in your body and your brain and growing is a tricky business. The human organism is fantastically complicated, full of breathtakingly sophisticated parts that all must work in harmony. For example, your brain, which is roughly three pounds of water, fat, and protein, has about 100 billion individual neurons, which do the "thinking," and another trillion glial cells, which help the neurons in their work. These cells operate in an environment so complex that the human brain has been called the most complicated object in the universe. Think about that the next time you look up into a starry night sky. There is nothing in our realm of knowledge that is more labyrinthine than our brain.

As we'll see in the pages ahead, the pathway to the maturity of your brain and body is long and winding, and full of both opportunities and hazards. As a parent—the big person taking care of the little person in your care—it's your job (a happy one, I hope) to help your child navigate the path and grow up to be strong, loving, and self-sufficient.

Your Body, Brain, and Hormones

As you grow from infancy to adulthood, and until the day you die, your brain and your body are inexorably bound together. What affects your brain will affect your body, and vice-versa. While the brain gives the orders that control the body, the body plays a big part in sending information to the brain and influencing its decisions.

One of the ways your brain organizes the functioning of your body is through hormones. These are chemicals produced by glands in your body that serve as messengers, traveling in your bloodstream to tissues and organs to direct them in their work. They affect many different processes, including growth and development, metabolism (how your body gets energy from the foods you eat), sexual function and reproduction, and your emotions. Their relationship with your brain is a two-way street, with influence going both ways.

Here are a few of the most important hormones.

Adrenaline—known as the "fight or flight" hormone. When you sense danger, it increases the metabolic rate and the dilation of blood vessels going to the heart and the brain. It also triggers some blood vessels to contract, to direct blood toward major muscle groups, including the heart and lungs. The increase of adrenaline will also decrease the body's ability to feel pain. Excessively high levels of adrenaline due to prolonged stress can cause heart damage, insomnia, and anxiety.

Cortisol—controls physical and psychological stress. When you're under duress, it increases heart rate, blood pressure, and respiration. Too much cortisol can lead to a condition called Cushing's syndrome. The symptoms of Cushing's syndrome include high blood pressure and mood swings, which show as anxiety, depression or irritability.

Estrogen—a female sex hormone released by the ovaries that's responsible for reproduction, menstruation, and menopause.

Insulin—allows the body to use glucose or sugar from carbohydrates in the food for energy, or to store glucose for future use. If you have type 2 diabetes—which is a growing epidemic—

then the cells in your body have become resistant to your body's natural insulin, leading to dangerously high levels of blood glucose.

Melatonin—regulates the sleep–wake cycle. Melatonin levels drop before you wake up, and rise when you go to sleep.

Serotonin—known as nature's feel-good chemical, it's associated with learning and memory, regulating sleep, digestion, mood, and some muscular functions.

Testosterone—the male sex hormone.

Why should you be concerned about levels of these hormones?

Because if they get out of balance, your mental and physical health can be negatively impacted.

Okay, but what does that have to do with how the big people treat you when you're a little kid?

Because of the disturbing experiences you have—at any age—can produce permanent physical changes in your body and brain.

Let that sink in for a minute.

Most people know that if something bad happens to you, such as a frightening experience, then certain hormones, particularly your adrenaline, surge. For a while, you feel "revved-up," in fight-or-flight mode. Then when the danger is passed, your hormones return to what's called homeostasis, which is defined as the "tendency toward a relatively stable equilibrium between interdependent elements, especially as maintained by physiological processes." Basically, you return to "normal," as if nothing ever happened, and you go on with your happy life.

But it's not that simple.

If you have a single truly terrifying experience or a series of stressful experiences, your hormones can become "stuck" in the fight-or-flight mode. They never return to their normal level. As a result, your body chemistry changes, and your brain can change too. You live in a state of perpetual discomfort. To relieve this discomfort, you may seek to self-medicate with drugs or alcohol or fatty foods.

There are various names for this syndrome. One of them is post-traumatic stress disorder (PTSD), which we see in military veterans and victims of violent crime. As the Mayo Clinic describes this disorder, PTSD is caused by a complex mix of:

1. Inherited mental health risks, such as a family history of anxiety and depression.

2. Inherited features of your personality—often called your temperament.

3. The way your brain regulates the chemicals and hormones your body releases in response to stress.

4. Stressful experiences, including the amount and severity of trauma you've gone through in your life.

The first two factors are inherited, and very difficult to change. Number three is also not under your conscious control. Number four—stressful experiences—may or may not be under your control, depending on the circumstances of your home life and career.

The parallel syndrome in children is called adverse childhood experiences, or ACEs.

Adverse Childhood Experiences (ACEs)

Adverse childhood experiences (ACEs) are traumatic or stressful events, including neglect and abuse, that occur to someone at the age of eighteen or younger. ACEs may be physical, such as being beaten or abused; emotional, such as being subjected to repeated parental scorn or verbal attacks; and otherwise traumatic, such as growing up with family members who have substance use disorders, or witnessing domestic or neighborhood violence.

Research has shown that instead of being harmless events that young people quickly put behind them, ACEs are strongly related to the development and persistence of a wide range of health problems throughout a person's lifespan, including those associated with substance misuse, depression, and suicide.

The first landmark ACE study was published in 1998 in the American Journal of Preventive Medicine. Conducted by Kaiser Permanente and the Centers for Disease Control and Prevention (CDC), it examined the records of over seventeen thousand commercially insured members on the short- and long-term impacts of childhood trauma.

The project was initiated to study the root causes of obesity, but as the research unfolded the scientists discovered something shocking: Among adults with chronic health problems, many also had high numbers of ACEs. These experiences were defined as parental substance abuse, childhood neglect, witnessing violence, and other catastrophic events.

The ACEs study found that 12.5 percent of the study participants had experienced four or more such events and that there was a "strong-dose response relationship between the number of childhood exposures and each of the ten risk factors for the leading cause of death." The term "dose–response relationship," or "exposure–response relationship," describes the change in effect on an organism caused by differing levels of exposure, or doses, to a stressor after a certain exposure time. For example, if you "dose" a child with a stressful and violent domestic episode, there will be a corresponding physiological effect on that child, which may last a lifetime.

According to the Centers for Disease Control and Prevention (CDC), there are four common types of abuse and neglect:

1. Physical abuse is the intentional use of physical force that can result in physical harm. Examples include hitting, kicking, shaking, burning, or other shows of force against a child.

2. Sexual abuse involves pressuring or forcing a child to engage in sexual acts. It includes behaviors such as fondling, penetration, and exposing a child to other sexual activities.

3. Emotional abuse refers to behaviors that harm a child's self-worth or emotional well-being. Examples include name-calling, shaming, rejection, withholding love, and threatening.

4. Neglect is the failure to meet a child's basic physical and emotional needs. These needs include housing, food, clothing, education, and access to medical care.

Another word for this syndrome is "toxic stress." As Dr. Heather Finlay-Morreale wrote in her 2019 paper "Adverse childhood experiences: How changing a child's environment can help," children who experience toxic stress are more likely to suffer from a host of ailments as they age. "Some are easy to link to childhood ACEs, such as mental health issues, obesity, or substance abuse," she wrote, "but even ailments that are viewed as more 'physical,' such as asthma, are increased. It has been shown that stress in childhood changes a person's body, mind—and even their DNA—in harmful ways."

Stress and Gene Expression

Can toxic stress actually alter your DNA?

In order to address this question, it's first a good idea to understand a few things about genetics.

Your DNA is the genetic code that determines who you are—human or monkey, tall or short, hairy or bald. In each cell of your body, you have about 3 billion DNA "base pairs," linked in the familiar ladder-like configuration.

In each of your trillions of cells, your DNA is packed into genes, with sections of DNA in each gene. For example, the gene for eye color contains the sections of DNA corresponding to eye color. You have between 20,000 and 25,000 genes.

Your genes are packaged into chromosomes. There are 24 distinct human chromosomes: 22 autosomal chromosomes, plus the sex-determining X and Y chromosomes.

The point of knowing this is that your DNA doesn't provide operating instructions directly to the larger organism; the blueprints must be "interpreted" by your genes. Think of your DNA as a book written in one language but read by people who speak a different language. The book must, therefore, be translated, and the translation will vary according to the local environment.

This interplay between DNA and the environment is what makes each person unique. For example, it accounts for the subtle differences between identical twins.

Epigenetics, meaning "attached to the DNA," is the study of such modifications. Scientists are discovering that not only can stress alter your gene expression—that is, how your DNA is interpreted by your genes—but can change the DNA itself. For example, research using mice (unlike human subjects, you can open them up and examine their brains) has shown that chronic exposure to corticosterone, a stress hormone, caused the mice to appear more anxious during a maze test.

They've also found that chronic exposure to corticosterone altered the expression of certain genes.

In a human gene called Fkbp5, genetic variations have been associated with post-traumatic stress disorder and mood disorders. If you think of the stress system as preparing you for fight or flight, it's theorized that these epigenetic changes might prepare you to fight harder or flee faster the next time you encounter something stressful. But modern humans aren't facing the occasional wild animal attack, requiring a vigorous physical response. Today's stressors, such as domestic violence or long-term emotional abuse, are things we can neither fight nor flee. Chronic stress may, therefore, lead to depression or other mood disorders.

The conclusion of much of the research being done today is that chronic exposure to stress hormones, whether occurring during the prenatal period, infancy, childhood, adolescence, adulthood, or aging, has a detrimental effect on brain structures involved in cognition and mental health. The specific effects on the brain and behavior emerge as a function of the timing and the duration of the exposure, as well as the interaction between gene effects and any previous exposure to environmental adversity.

A particularly poignant example of the relationship between childhood stress and adult psychiatric problems, including suicide, can be seen in the unfortunate case of the renowned musician Kurt Cobain. While we have not analyzed his epigenetic profile, his suicide in 1994 at the age of twenty-seven came after a lifetime of family stress. When Cobain was nine years old, his parents divorced. He later said that the divorce had a profound effect on his life. His mother noted that his personality changed dramatically, and her son became defiant and withdrawn. In a 1993 interview with British journalist John Savage, Cobain said:

"I remember feeling ashamed, for some reason. I was ashamed of my parents. I couldn't face some of my friends at school anymore, because I desperately wanted to have the classic, you know, typical family. Mother, father. I wanted that security, so I resented my parents for quite a few years because of that."

During his adolescence, two of Kurt's uncles committed suicide with guns. Research shows that exposure to suicide in the family increases the risk to a child who is depressed, possibly because suicide is seen as an acceptable or possible thing to do. After Kurt shot himself, his cousin Beverly Cobain, a registered nurse, and mental health professional, told Brian Libby from HealthDay, "Alcoholism runs rampant in the Cobain family. When I was growing up there was always alcohol and violence in our home." She said that Kurt was diagnosed at a young age with attention deficit disorder (ADD), then later with bipolar disorder. "His risk was very high," she told Libby. "Untreated bipolar disorder, drug addiction, prior suicides of family members, alcohol, violence, and unpredictability in his childhood, poor self-esteem, violence in his married life. Kurt could have been a poster child for risk of suicide."

Not every child who experiences family stress or abuse is permanently altered, but enough are negatively affected that it's become an accepted axiom of behavioral science. The old saying, "As the twig is bent, so shall grow the tree" is very true, and something that every parent needs to take to heart.

Chapter 2: Creating an Autonomous Environment

Here are two statements that are each absolutely true.

1. The *problem* with children is that they have minds of their own, and insist on doing what they want.

2. The *blessing* of children is that they have minds of their own, and insist on doing what they want.

This is not a new conundrum. I invite you to pick up a copy of the Bible and thumb your way to the Book of Genesis, where God—the overworked single parent of Adam and Eve—is irritated by his children's newfound sense of independence and self-direction. Seeing they each have minds of their own, he says to them, "Okay, if you're so smart, you can get out of Eden and fend for yourselves in the cruel real world." But of course, any theologian will tell you that by only exercising their free will did Adam and Eve became fully human, with all the satisfaction and hardship that comes with the position.

In my years of practice, I have yet to meet an American parent who wanted their child to be a robot. By "robot" I mean a dutiful child who does exactly what he or she is told, and nothing more or nothing less. A child who has no imagination takes no risks and finds no joy in exploring the unknown.

As parents, we value and reward personal characteristics such as respect for elders, the ability and willingness to follow the rules, and knowledge of the established ways of the world. But we also claim to admire those children—and adults—who soar above the crowd, blaze their own trail, and even—most breathtakingly—surpass the achievements of their parents. Sometimes we express enthusiasm for such children in *theory*, but not in *reality*. We say, "Oh, look at the Smith boy! He's such an achiever! He has a summer job and is planning to go to college!" But when it comes to assessing the progress of our own children, suddenly it gets *personal*. We judge their successes or failures as if they were our own. And too often, we encourage them to play it safe and not take chances. We say to them, "Learn from me and my painful experience. What you want to do is foolish. I want to save you from the pain of having to learn for yourself that your choice will lead to disappointment. Stick with the tried and true. Don't go out on a limb. It's too risky."

We give life to our children, but then we want to keep them from experiencing life to its fullest.

We Are Not Puppets of the Universe

I've met many parents who have an attitude of fatalism. They believe their lives are fundamentally not under their control, and it's hopeless to try to defy the hand of fate. Some parents overtly say to their children, "It's God's will that such-and-such should happen, and we should not try to do otherwise." They believe that good things cannot happen to them, and therefore if something positive happens—their adult child gets a promotion at work or meets a terrific love interest—it must be a cruel trick, and those bad things will surely follow as compensation.

Many parents lack confidence in their own abilities to manage their children's lives. They don't have a clear roadmap, and consequently are too controlling of their children by not allowing and encouraging them to explore their environment. This begins when the baby first develops the ability to sit upright without assistance, grasp objects and place them in their mouths, crawl, and ultimately walk. Instead of being delighted by these signs of human intelligence, many parents harshly punish and criticize their children for having normal innate curiosity about their environment and acting on their curiosity. Such severe treatment results in children becoming afraid to explore their surroundings, not knowing when they will be hit, screamed at, and criticized.

Like the unformed human dropped onto the planet in the beginning of this book, such children eventually suspect that they are being punished *simply for existing*. What thought could be more depressing?

This "not knowing" can develop into crippling self-doubt. Criticism, and in severe cases derogatory name-calling, results in shame. If these parental behaviors continue, the child feels inadequacy and doubt throughout childhood and into adulthood. It's a form of abuse that provokes a very real stress response in the child. If it's sustained and severe, the child's hormones can be permanently altered and the "set point' of homeostasis—what is "normal" for the child's biochemistry—can be set to a different and damaging level. The child becomes an adolescent and even an adult with a built-in case of PTSD that's not much different from those seen in military veterans.

As the result of severe or sustained adverse childhood experiences in the form of aggressive parental suppression, the child becomes an adult with anxiety regarding trying new things or thinking differently from his or her parents. Or, the child feels angry from the cruel treatment and becomes hostile and aggressive toward his or her parents, and often times develops a hatred for authority figures which ranges from parents to teachers, pastors and preachers, school principals, and police officers, and ultimately a disdain for rules, regulations, and laws.

Developing Autonomy

Autonomy means self-governing and functioning independently. Erik Erikson, the 20th- century German-American developmental psychologist and psychoanalyst known for his theory on the psychological development of human beings, and who is perhaps most famous for coining the phrase "identity crisis," focused on healthy personality development. This was opposed to Sigmund Freud's idea that healthy emotional growth occurred through treating and curing neurotic behavior. Erikson's theory of healthy child development suggested that each child passes through a series of psychosocial stages. They are:

Stage 1 - Trust vs. Mistrust

Stage 2 - Autonomy vs. Shame and Doubt

Stage 3 - Initiative vs. Guilt

Stage 4 - Industry vs. Inferiority

Stage 5 - Identity vs. Confusion

Stage 6 - Intimacy vs. Isolation

Stage 7 - Generativity vs. Stagnation

Stage 8 - Integrity vs. Despair

For example, during the first stage, Trust vs. Mistrust, the child learns whether or not they can trust the world—specifically, their parents and other caregivers on whom they depend for food and shelter. For example, when the baby cries, does her caregiver attend to her needs? When he is hungry, does he receive nourishment from his caregivers? If the answer is "yes," then the child trusts that the world is a fair and affirmative place where you find love. If the answer is "no," the child learns the world is not to be trusted, is unfair, and is a place where you cannot expect to be loved. This is an unhealthy condition of constant stress—and we have seen what that can do to a growing brain and developing body.

The second stage, Autonomy vs. Shame and Doubt, corresponds to a toddler between the ages of two and three, and centers around the question, "Can I do things myself, or am I wholly reliant on the help of others?" This question mainly focuses on bowel and bladder control—that is to say, toilet training. Other important events include gaining more control over food choices, toy preferences, and clothing selection.

I believe that Autonomy versus Shame and Doubt should be applied throughout childhood, beginning with the child's earliest development of motility, which is approximately two months old, when he or she begins to grasp objects and wants to place them in their mouth. Creating an autonomous environment begins with the mindset of you, the parents. You should be aware of the "developmental push" which occurs innately within the infant and encourage and promote this natural phenomenon. Allow the infant to grip your finger, clutch a teddy bear or a blanket, smell your cologne or perfume, play with your hair.

As the infant grows, encourage safe exploration without punishment. Allow them to crawl, touch things, and physically feel the hardness of the floor and the softness of a pillow. Encourage the toddler to know that exploring the home is safe, fun, and exciting!

No need for criticism or slapping the child's hand for accidentally knocking over a cup of water at the dinner table. We can laugh and say, "That was an accident, that's all," and clean it up.

No need to spank a toddler for crayon drawings on the bedroom wall. We say, "Let's draw on paper instead," and you both make cleaning the wall together a fun activity. One day, he or she will know to draw on paper and not the wall and will do such independently.

No need for constant direction from the parents. Creating an autonomous environment means you allow your child to experience life and explore without fear. Applying this mindset throughout childhood promotes healthy self-esteem and empathy, independent thinking, problem-solving, and a curiosity for exploring the world. It also reduces stress so that emotionally or physically challenging events—like falling off your bike or getting picked on at school—are transitory, not permanent, thereby allowing the hormonal "fight or flight" response to subside back to a healthy level.

This Does Not Mean Let Your Child Run Wild

"Autonomous" does not mean "feral." Human beings live in communities and families with highly developed structures and social norms, and any parent who lets their child be a "free spirit" or doesn't want to "put them in a box" runs the risk of raising a future adult who doesn't know how to interact with other people and may run afoul of the law.

Children of all ages need boundaries, not to suffocate them but to direct their growth and energy in a positive direction. Without an adequate and reasonable exposure to rules and boundaries at home, a child will have difficulty dealing with the rules and boundaries encountered at school. And if—for some reason—they aren't exposed to boundaries at school, then they are more likely to fail when navigating the rules and boundaries encountered when they eventually enter society at large.

Across the spectrum of parents, there will be varying degrees of the autonomy versus control they seek to establish and enforce for their children. The amount of control parents want to exert depends on many variables, including:

- Religious beliefs
- Beliefs about the role of the individual in society
- Physical location of the home—on a safe suburban cul-de-sac or in a dangerous inner-city apartment block
- Age and temperament of the child
- Resources available for supervision
- Local laws and customs

The Bare Minimum

At the very least, you need to keep your child in a safe enough environment so that you don't run afoul of local laws and the department of social services.

An easy example is the use of child safety seats in automobiles. It may be hard to believe, but these ubiquitous car accessories were not widely mandated until 1985. Before then, and particularly before seat belts were federally mandated for all automobiles in 1968, kids were just herded into the family station wagon any which way, or allowed to bump along in the back of the pickup truck. I can remember lounging around in the flat back area of the family's Ford Country Squire station wagon as the big V-8 engine rocketed us down the highway at seventy miles an hour!

Those were the days when the death rate from auto accidents was truly horrific, and we've come a long way since, but we can do better. According to the Centers for Disease Control (CDC) and the National Highway Traffic Administration, in the United States during 2016, 723 children ages twelve years and younger died as occupants in motor vehicle crashes, and more than 128,000 were injured.

One CDC study found that, in one year, more than 618,000 children aged infant to twelve rode in vehicles without the use of a child safety seat or booster seat or a seat belt at least some of the time. Of the children ages, twelve years and younger who died in a crash in 2016 (for which restraint use was known), 35 percent were *not* buckled up.

These days, putting a child in the seat of a car between the ages of eight and twelve, and then in a seat/shoulder belt, is a standard and ubiquitous practice carried out by even the most freedom-loving parents.

At the minimum, you need to provide a clean and safe home environment for your child. If you or your family become involved with your local department of social services (or child welfare, or any one of many other names), you'll soon know about home inspections by DSS representatives. In North Carolina, where I practice, we have a federally mandated, state-supervised, county-administered social services system. This means the federal government authorizes national programs and a majority of the funding, and the state provides oversight and support. In North Carolina, the single administrative agency is the NC Department of Health and Human Services (DHHS). The 100 local social service agencies (mine is Wake County, home of the city of Raleigh) deliver the services and benefits.

North Carolina state law requires that all counties provide Child Protective Services (CPS) to ensure that children are safe and that their basic needs are being met. This is true for all families regardless of income or if they are involved with other programs at the Department of Social Services. Child Protective Services is:

• Legally mandated for children alleged to be abused, neglected, and/or dependent, and who are at imminent risk of harm due to actions by the child's parent or caretaker

• Designed to protect children from further harm and improve parental/caretaker abilities in order to assure a safe and nurturing home for each child

I know this sounds extreme—I'm sure you'd never allow your child's environment to fall below CPS standards—but for some families, for various reasons these minimal standards need to be learned and enforced.

In the next chapter, we'll discuss some specific steps you should take to make your child's environment safe for autonomy. This means safe for exploration, fun, and learning, without the child feeling as though they're in a prison.

Chapter 3: Balancing Safety and Freedom

If you're reading this book, you have concerns and questions about the best way to raise your child—either now or in the future—and you want to strike a happy balance between protecting your child from obvious dangers and allowing him or her to take safe risks and get a few skinned knees in the process.

You do not want your child to handle a rattlesnake, but you're happy to take them to a zoo to see one behind glass, and to learn about snakes and how they live.

Let's start with your home environment. You need to undertake basic *due diligence*, which means eliminating the most common household dangers. These simple steps will allow you, the overworked parent, to relax in your own home without experiencing constant anxiety about your child's every move.

I don't want to scare you, but child safety is an important matter because kids really do get hurt—and even killed—in household accidents. As the CDC reported in 2008, among children in the United States, unintentional injuries—such as those caused by burns, drowning, falls, poisoning, and road traffic—are *the leading cause of morbidity and mortality*. Each year, among kids aged birth to nineteen years of age, more than 12,000 die from unintentional injuries and more than 9.2 million are treated in emergency departments for nonfatal injuries.

Among children, the leading causes of death are motor vehicles in traffic, pedestrian and pedal cyclist accidents, suffocation (among infants), and drowning.

Nonfatal injuries are most commonly caused by falls, being struck by or against an object, animal bites or insect stings, and poisoning.

Among children and teens, another significant cause of death is firearms. At this time, thanks to the 1996 federal Dickey Amendment, there's no comprehensive or recent federal data on gun-related injuries or deaths—and that includes from the CDC. But independent data sources suggest firearms are the second leading cause of death among American children and adolescents, after car crashes. Firearm deaths occur at a rate more than three times higher than drownings. According to TheTrace.org, in the United States, middle- and high-school-age children are now more likely to die as the result of a firearm injury than from any other single cause of death.

I'll talk more about firearm safety in the pages ahead.

Here's a checklist of items that you'll want to bring into line with home safety standards.

Physical Safety—Baby

When you first bring your baby home, controlling your child will seem super-easy because infants aren't mobile. When you put them somewhere, they tend to stay there. They may roll over, but that's about it. They are cute and inert.

Around six to nine months, your life will change because your baby will start crawling. Then sometime between nine and twelve months, they'll begin to walk, and by the time they're fifteen months old may be highly ambulatory. If you're a first-time parent, this can be a rude awakening. Now you've got a tiny, walking, grabbing, inquisitive human roaming your house who *does not respond to verbal commands!* They have minimal speech skills, so telling them to cease and desist is a waste of time. You have to save that for when they start understanding conversations, which is about the age of two. (Remember, every child is different; these are only averages.) It's also at the age of two or three that kids become capable of self-directed play—they'll busy themselves with a toy or a drawing for a few minutes at a time, which is a big relief to the beleaguered parent.

Get ahead of the game. Take the necessary steps to ensure your baby's safety from day one, and then as time passes, you'll notice any danger areas that need attention. Here are the basics, adapted from guidelines by the U.S. Department of Health & Human Services:

- Cover all unused electrical sockets with plastic outlet plugs.
- Keep all types of cords out of baby's reach, including curtain cords. Move furniture, lamps, and electronics to hide electrical cords.

- Secure furniture and electronics, including bookcases and TVs, so your child cannot pull them down. If you live in an earthquake zone, you should have done this already.
- Install safety gates at the bottom and top of staircases. Close doors to unsafe rooms, such as the laundry room.
- Look around for sharp edges at baby's level, such as the coffee table. When your baby stands up, they can easily bang their head—you have to watch out for this.
- Store all cleaning products, medicines, and other poisons out of baby's reach.
- Get safety latches for kitchen and bathroom cabinet doors that the baby can reach.
- Keep houseplants out of baby's reach. Some plants can poison or make your baby sick, and your baby can make a huge mess out of them.
- Set your water heater temperature to no higher than 125 degrees Fahrenheit. Water that is hotter can cause serious burns.
- Closely supervise your baby around the family pet. Toddlers have no empathy and will blithely treat the cat the same way they treat their raggedy old doll.

As your baby becomes a child, you'll need to keep pace with their increasing capabilities and needs for new experiences. Don't worry—while it may seem like a lot to keep track of, after a while you'll get used to running through your mental checklist of home and outdoor hazards. Each time your child reaches a new age milestone or enters a new environment, you'll be able to scan the environment and the computer in your brain will flash a warning if you see anything questionable.

Physical Safety—Childhood

This is not intended to be a comprehensive list of every hazard a child can face at home or on the playground. It's intended to help you think about the possibilities and plan for unfortunate possibilities.

• Ensure windows and screens are secure, especially if the child lives on or has access to an upper floor. Tragic accidents can happen. In 1991, Conor Clapton, the 4 1/2-year-old son of the rock guitarist Eric Clapton, was killed when he fell from an open bedroom window on the 53rd floor of a Manhattan apartment building. Police said the window, about six feet high and four feet wide, was left open after it was cleaned by a housekeeper. The boy, who was not in the room during the cleaning, darted past the housekeeper and somehow fell out the window, which was not protected by a window guard.

• Check the swing set, slide, and other outdoor play gear for sturdiness, rust, splinters, and sharp edges.

• Make sure surface beneath the swing set is soft enough to absorb the shock of a fall.

• Ensure that outdoor toys are put away in a secure place when not in use.

- Pool safety is critical! You need climb-proof fencing at least five feet (1.5 meters) high on all sides of the pool. There may be local laws mandating pool fencing. But remember—even little children can climb fences. In 2014, three-year-old Edward Harris slipped away from family members at a daycare center on Staten Island, climbed over a fence, and fell into an above ground pool, where he was found moments later—but tragically, it was too late.
- Make sure the pool fence has a self-closing gate with a childproof lock, and a cover when not in use. If the pool can be accessed through a door to the house, have a door alarm installed.

Gun Safety

Many people own guns for sport and to protect themselves and their families. But with kids in the house, there's a risk of a tragic accident. According to WRAL.com in Raleigh, North Carolina—my hometown—statistics show a gun in the home is 43 times more likely to kill a family member or friend than kill an intruder in self-defense.

According to a Rutgers University report on ScienceDaily.com, for all children aged one to seventeen, injuries from firearms are the third leading cause of death. They are also responsible for thousands of children being treated for open wounds, fractures, and brain and spinal injuries. "In addition," the article notes, "children who witness firearm injury can experience psychological effects, such as fear, anxiety, and elevated stress." It's true—firearm violence can be a form of adverse childhood experience that can result in lifelong changes to gene expression.

Keep your guns locked up and the ammunition stored separately. State laws vary considerably, so be sure you know yours, especially if you're a new arrival.

In North Carolina, no current law penalizes home storage unless a child under the age of twelve actually gets possession of a loaded gun for a proscribed purpose:

North Carolina Laws § 14-315.1. Storage of firearms to protect minors.

(a) Any person who resides in the same premises as a minor, owns or possesses a firearm, and stores or leaves the firearm (i) in a condition that the firearm can be discharged and (ii) in a manner that the person knew or should have known that an unsupervised minor would be able to gain access to the firearm, is guilty of a Class 1 misdemeanor if a minor gains access to the firearm without the lawful permission of the minor's parents or a person having charge of the minor, and the minor:

(1) Possesses it in violation of G.S. 14-269.2(b);

(2) Exhibits it in a public place in a careless, angry, or threatening manner;

(3) Causes personal injury or death with it, not in self-defense; or

(4) Uses it in the commission of a crime.

In contrast, Massachusetts is currently the only state that requires that all firearms be stored with a locking device in place when the firearms are not in use:

Massachusetts General Laws c.140 § 131L

It shall be unlawful to store or keep any firearm, rifle or shotgun including, but not limited to, large capacity weapons, or machine gun in any place unless such weapon is secured in a locked container or equipped with a tamper-resistant mechanical lock or other safety device, properly engaged so as to render such weapon inoperable by any person other than the owner or other lawfully authorized user. It shall be unlawful to store or keep any stun gun in any place unless such weapon is secured in a locked container accessible only to the owner or other lawfully authorized user. For purposes of this section, such weapon shall not be deemed stored or kept if carried by or under the control of the owner or other lawfully authorized user.

Penalties are stiff—a fine and a prison term for merely storing the firearm improperly. If the firearm happens to be a large capacity firearm or machine gun, stored or kept in a place where a person younger than 18 years of age may have access without committing an unforeseeable trespass, the penalty is a fine of not less than $10,000 nor more than $20,000, or by imprisonment for not less than 4 years nor more than 15 years, or by both such fine and imprisonment.

"Stranger Danger": Use Facts, Not Fear

It seems like every day you see on the news or in a re-run of *Law & Order* that a child has been abducted. It seems like an epidemic, and while the phrase "stranger danger" is catchy and seems to say all you need to know, the reality is much more complicated. It's not simply a matter of telling your children all strangers are bad and nothing more. In fact, the idea of stranger danger is vastly overblown; the majority of child abductions and sexual abuse cases are not committed by strangers, and most missing children are not victims of abduction but runaways. As a parent concerned with your child's safety, you need a more comprehensive approach that goes beyond stranger danger to teach your child to recognize suspicious behaviors regardless of the context.

"The most important thing that parents need to know," explains Elizabeth Jeglic, Ph.D., a professor of psychology at the City University of New York Graduate Center, and author of *Protecting Your Child from Sexual Abuse*, "is that ninety-three percent of sexual abuse against children is perpetrated by those known to the child—meaning family, friends, and those they know in their environment, like teachers and coaches." As she told Matthew Utley from Fatherly.com, "We are targeting the wrong individuals when we teach our children about stranger danger. We are better off teaching our children about consent and that no one should be touching them without their permission."

Of course, when your children are dealing with strangers, you need to teach them the two foundational rules:

1. Don't accept rides from strangers, regardless of the person's enticing or plausible story ("Your mom sent me to pick you up," "I'm looking for my lost puppy," etc.).

2. Don't open the door for a stranger. If someone knocks, get an adult.

But you should go a step further and remember that offenders can be just about anyone. A third of abusive acts perpetrated against minors are committed by another minor, and sometimes even by a girl. Statistics say 93 percent of childhood sexual abuse is committed by an adult known to the child. This is an area that you need to supervise because if Dirty Uncle molests Johnny, he will admonish the child to say nothing and keep the incident a secret. Instead of telling you, Johnny might very well keep his mouth shut, and instead develop symptoms of post-traumatic stress disorder, for which you will have no explanation. The toxic effects of both secret and overt sexual abuse can surface later in life; as numerous studies have shown, there is increasing evidence that adverse childhood experiences such as childhood abuse may be implicated in the development of serious psychological issues.

For example, researchers Penelope K. Trickett and colleagues reported in "The impact of sexual abuse on female development: Lessons from a multigenerational, longitudinal research study," sexually abused females show negative psychological characteristics in many areas including earlier onsets of puberty, depression, dissociative symptoms, maladaptive sexual development, high rates of obesity, more major illnesses and healthcare utilization, dropping out of high school, persistent post-traumatic stress disorder, self-mutilation, physical and sexual revictimization, drug and alcohol abuse, and domestic violence.

Listen to your child! If your child says they don't want to be touched, either in a tickle fight or when they meet Aunt Millie, you need to respect that. If your child seems reluctant or fearful to have Cousin Eddie act as caregiver while you're out for the evening, gently—and in private—find out why. If your child dreads going to the church overnight camp, even if you're afraid to offend the kindly pastor, encourage your child to talk to you about it. The hardest thing to do is contradict the assumption that the adult who is a respected member of the community could never harm a child. Sad to say, sometimes these pillars of the community turn out to be predators.

Keeping your child safe at home, school, and in the neighborhood should include vigilance against "stranger danger," but must also include your own awareness and willingness to investigate situations that seem "off" to you, especially if your child—verbally or through their emotional responses—sends a signal to you that something is making them fearful or conflicted.

Don't Keep Your Child Isolated

On the flip side, overprotection is not the answer. To learn about their behavior, your child needs to co-exist with other people. I'm sure you've heard the term "street smarts." Well, you don't acquire street smarts by never going out on the street.

I once had a friend who had two children, a girl, and a boy, five years apart. When Jane was born, my friend and his wife lived in a rough area in the South End section of Boston. Their apartment was on a major thoroughfare, and there was gang activity in the area. Jane attended preschool about two miles from her home, and her parents did not own a car (not unusual among city dwellers). To go to preschool, Jane and her mom rode the bus. To go shopping, they took the subway downtown.

Because of their urban location, Jane, who was always accompanied by one parent or the other, quickly learned about all the "characters" who lived in the South End. She learned how to ride the bus and the subway. She developed a sense of how to handle creepy people, as well as get along with the nice ones.

When Jane was six years old and her brother Joey was one, the family left the city and moved to the suburbs. In their new neighborhood, there was no bus, no subway, no local "characters." They were glad to be out of the city. They drove everywhere and had carefully arranged play dates for Joey. At night their street was quiet—no sirens or boom boxes, like there had been in the South End.

As Jane grew up in her new suburban home, she exhibited a real knack for navigating her way among people, both her peers and adults. In high school, she was elected senior class president, and then she decided to go to college in New York City. After graduation, she became a successful marketing executive in Los Angeles.

Joey did fine, too, but he's not a "people person." He works as an arborist, among trees, with a small team of colleagues. He feels uncomfortable in the city and goes downtown as rarely as possible.

It's interesting how as they grow up, kids gravitate to the environments that make them feel most comfortable. Sadly, if a child has been abused, he or she will do exactly that. But what will give them comfort may be drug abuse, anorexia, alcohol, obesity—any number of methods by which they can self-medicate and make the pain go away. Because that's exactly what these diseases are: attempts to ease the pain that lingers inside and never goes away.

When compared to adults who have never been sexually abused, a sexually abused child or young adult has a greater chance of becoming obese or having psychiatric issues later in life. As researcher Danielle L. Gabert and colleagues reported in "Prevalence and Predictors of Self-Reported Sexual Abuse in Severely Obese Patients in a Population-Based Bariatric Program," in their study of five hundred patients enrolled in an obesity program, "the prevalence of self-reported sexual abuse was 21.8 percent, and psychosocial issues such as addiction and psychiatric illnesses were the major independent predictors of abuse." Abused patients, who were more likely to be women than men, reported significant impairments in health status compared to those not abused.

Food Safety

It's interesting that many parents take great care to create a safe physical and emotional environment for their child, only to stock the refrigerator with "food products" that are minimally nutritious and have a long-term negative effect on health.

What good is it, one may ask, to protect a child from broken bones or common colds—which are temporary afflictions—while exposing them to the lifelong harm of junk food?

Granted, all across the globe, you'll find parents who have all sorts of ideas about nutrition and proper diets. Nutrition and food are some of the most complex aspects of human lives, being influenced by biochemical, psychological, social, and cultural factors. But it cannot be denied that the "Western diet," mainly characterized by the intake of large amounts of red meat, dairy products, refined grains, and sugar, positively correlates to acne, obesity, diabetes, heart disease, and cancer, the so-called "diseases of civilization". And according to the 2015–2020 Dietary Guidelines for Americans, more than two-thirds of American adults and nearly one-third of children and youth are overweight or obese. Half of American adults have one or more diet-related chronic diseases such as heart disease, high blood pressure, type 2 diabetes, and certain cancers.

Sadly, many of these diseases first take root in childhood. That's not what anyone would call health safety.

The problem, say, scientists, is that the Western diet emerged during the Industrial Revolution and accelerated at the end of the 20th century, but our genetic makeup, and how our bodies process food, has been unchanged for millions of years. The evolutionary collision of our ancient genome with the nutritional qualities of recently introduced foods may underlie many of the chronic diseases of Western civilization.

You can take steps to lower your child's risk of obesity, heart disease, and other ailments associated with our modern diet.

• Start teaching healthy eating habits early. Train your kids to eat healthily and model that behavior yourself. You probably wouldn't smoke a cigarette in front of your child, so why eat junk food? Show your kids what good eating habits look like.

• Keep your kids healthy with more plant-based foods—vegetables and fruit (which are high in fiber), legumes, herbs and spices, and whole grains instead of refined grains.

• Give them less salt and sugar. Currently, 90 percent of Americans consume more than the daily recommended amount of sodium, according to the CDC. The same goes for sugar, where the average American consumes more than three times as much sugar every day than is recommended.

• Choose healthy fats found in foods including salmon and oils from plants including canola, corn, olive, peanut, and sunflower, as well as some nuts and seeds.

• Choose minimally processed foods that don't contain many ingredients.

Above all, make time to sit down as a family to eat a home-cooked meal. This not only sets a great example for kids about the importance of healthy food, but it can also bring a family together—even the most rebellious teenager appreciates a tasty, home-cooked meal.

Regular family meals give your kids an opportunity to see you eating healthy food while keeping your portions in check and limiting junk food. They provide comfort and a sense of security, and an opportunity for you to catch up on your kids' daily lives.

Chapter 4: Healthy Parental Responses

Remember I began the book by asking you to imagine you've been dropped onto a strange planet about which you know nothing. And I didn't mean only that you knew nothing about the language or the topography or how you were going to support yourself. Those are skills and information you can easily learn as you go along. What's really important is that you find yourself under the care and protection of the big hairy people, who for the most part seem loving and eager to help you. But they also seem to have all sorts of rules by which they want you to live, and sometimes these rules are hard to figure out. Some of the rules seem designed only to make life less fun for you, but since the big people have physical control over you, for the most part, you do your best to keep them happy. The best way to do this, you learn, is by emulating their behavior. After all, they must know the best way to live, right? You eat what they eat, and you go where they go. You avoid the dangerous things they avoid. It makes sense that if you mimic their habits, you've got a good chance of surviving.

Once in a while, by accident or intent, you break the rules your parents have put into place. Their response to your transgression will be very informative and provide a direction for your future behavior.

Let's say you're in the house one day and, feeling particularly exuberant, you start running from room to room. Perhaps you're also chasing the dog, which makes the game even more fun. As you run from room to room, chasing the dog, you slip on the carpet and whack your head against a table. The table shakes and a vase falls over onto the floor and breaks. You cry out in pain because your head really hurts. You reach up to rub the sore spot and you see a little smear of blood on your hand. Wow! It's not just a little bump, but a real cut.

Your parent (mom or dad—either one) hears the commotion and rushes to the room.

By this time, you've lived on the planet long enough to know that running in the house and breaking the vase are *not* things your parents like. In fact, you remember being told not to run in the house because you could 1) get hurt or 2) break something. Well, now you've managed to do both at one time.

As your parent rushes to the scene of the accident/crime, what do you think her response is going to be?

1) She yells, "Do you know how much that vase cost me?" She calls you stupid, hits you, and tells you to get the hell up to your room, you little brat.

2) Throws up her hands and screams, "Just wait until your father gets home!"

3) Demands to know why you didn't listen to her because she's told you a million times not to run in the house. Makes it clear

it's your fault for breaking the vase and hitting your head. She does this as she takes you by the hand and leads you into the bathroom to examine your cut.

4) Picks you up, kisses you, and gently looks at your head. Takes you into the bathroom to get it cleaned up. After she thinks you're going to be okay, takes you back to the broken vase and says, "Well, we've got quite a mess to clean up, don't we? Would you please get me the broom and the dustpan? After we take care of this, we'll talk about running in the house. Perhaps you need to spend more time outside playing."

The Parents' Response Provides a Lesson

As the newcomer to the planet who's eager to learn the rules of the road, you're going to closely watch the response your parent gives to the accident/crime. Each reaction will carry its own lesson.

From the first scenario, you will learn: The strong rule over the weak. Anger is the appropriate response when you are displeased. Material objects (the vase) are more valuable than a person (or at least, your aching head). When someone has made a mistake, criticize and ostracize them. Your parent has a low opinion of you, which must mean that you're a bad person.

From the second scenario, you will learn: Dodging responsibility is one of the most unpleasant and disturbing things a parent can do. Your mother has chosen to make dad the enforcer, which means that when he comes home, she will pounce upon him and tell him to punish you. He'll be irritated at being cast in the role of the bad guy, and your parents may argue, which will make you feel guilty for having brought misery to the house. You will try to hide until it blows over and will have learned nothing constructive.

From the third scenario, you will learn: People respond to transgressions emotionally and put their own perspective above the bigger picture. You didn't listen to mother when she told you not to run in the house, so perhaps something is wrong with you. If you get hurt, the circumstances of *how* you got hurt will influence the parental response. If you get hurt while doing nothing wrong, you'll get more sympathy than for the exact same injury sustained while doing something bad.

From the fourth scenario, you will learn: Your mother must love you a lot because it was your welfare that first came to her mind. You were her priority. Then, when you felt better, she asked you to participate in cleaning up the broken vase. That seemed fair enough. And then—unlike the mothers in the first three scenarios—she offered to think about a positive solution for the problem of running in the house. If running outside is good and running inside is bad, then obviously the solution is to ensure the active child has plenty of opportunities to run outside.

If the vase needed to be replaced, would it be fair for your mother to ask you to contribute to get a new one? Sure—why not? But such a solution needs to be short and decisive.

If you're the parent, and the child has a nickel, then ask for the nickel. Or ask for a chore, like sweeping the walkway. Whatever it is, the punishment must be *immediate, realistic, and certain*. The worst thing you can say is, "You'll pay me a nickel every week for a month." To a child, a month is a lifetime. By tomorrow the child will have moved on to other things. After a week, the punishment will bear no relationship to the original mistake, and will simply feel like needless cruelty. Both praise and punishment should be delivered promptly and with love, and then life goes on.

When Your Child Crosses the Line, First Get the Facts

Sometimes a child will do something unsafe or ill-advised out of sight of the parent. This happens with increasing frequency as the child gets older and into their teens because they're spending more time autonomously, away from the parent. Look at it this way: If you have a child who is three years old, you likely know *everything* the child knows. This is because the child is with you every moment, or else in a structured environment such as a daycare center where you know the activities and the routine. Every experience your child has, you have also. You see what they see and hear what they hear.

But as your child becomes more independent, he or she will spend increasing amounts of time away from you and will have experiences with which you know nothing.

This is why I would recommend that if your child does anything that seems inappropriate, your first task is *not* to correct them. Your first job is to *investigate*, and to do this you need to get answers from the person who's in trouble: your child.

Let's say your daughter, a high school senior, comes home at midnight, and she's drunk.

What do you think is the *first thing* you should say? (Pick one):

A. "You're grounded for a month! Go to bed!"
B. "You were with those *bad kids*, weren't you? *They* got you drunk!"
C. "How could you do this to me? I try so hard to raise you properly!"
D. "Sit down. Have a glass of water. Tell me where you've been."

The answer is "D." Your first task is to get *information*, and to do this you need to be nice. If you start yelling, your child isn't going to tell you anything.

Say, "Okay, you've had a lot to drink. You're home now. Where did you go? Did you have fun? Did you drive? (I hope not!)." The worst thing you can do is blame *those other bad kids*. Why? Because your child chose to associate with them and play beer pong until they all got sick. Your child is responsible for his or her own choices. By blaming the bad kids, you're only insulting your child.

After you've had a nice, friendly discussion, and you've shown you respect your child, *then* you can say, "For the rest of the week, I think you need to stay home at night. I want you to focus on other things besides going out to parties. You need to take a step back."

By initially investigating rather than judging, you haven't given up your prerogative to exert parental authority. You can pass sentence any time you want. It's better to first *learn* about your child and his or her choices, and then hand down the punishment.

Keep Your Eye on the Goal

When you discipline your child, remember your ultimate goal:

You want your child to become an adult who is happy, loving, self-sufficient, and engaged in life.

Therefore, doesn't it make sense that at every learning opportunity (that is, when your child chases the dog and breaks the vase), your response should be geared towards achieving that goal? Of course. Therefore, it would be counterproductive to deliver a response that makes your child bitter, angry, resentful, or incapable of self-sufficient behavior. Instead, you want to focus on what the child *should* be doing. Always provide a positive alternative to negative behavior.

Say, "You've got a lot of energy! Instead of breaking vases, how about helping me to rake the lawn?" Whenever you remove a negative behavior, offer a positive behavior in its place. It's only human nature—if you say, "You should not do that," you're not offering a path forward. If you say, "*This* is what you should do," you're showing the child the road to the future.

We All Make Mistakes

One of the greatest lessons in life is that we will all make mistakes. Mistakes are a part of what it means to be human. (Just think of Adam and Eve. Pretty much the very first thing they did as living creatures was to make a big mistake and get tossed out of the Garden of Eden.) So, if as humans we are fated to make mistakes, then clearly there must be a best-practice solution for how to resolve them. This best-practice solution is as follows:

1) Admit the mistake, both to yourself and to those affected.

2) Apologize to those affected.

3) Offer to rectify the mistake as much as you can.

4) Think of how you could have better handled the circumstances leading up to the mistake.

5) Having learned something, then turn the page. Move on. Leave guilt behind.

When Johnny (or Suzy) chases the dog and knocks over the vase, as a parent you have the opportunity to point him towards the ultimate goal, which is to become an adult who is happy, loving, self-sufficient, and engaged in life. Going through the steps, you:

1) In a calm, loving voice, ask Johnny if he did it. He will say, "Yes. With the dog." (The qualifier is probably inevitable, but at least Johnny fessed up.)

2) Nicely ask him to apologize. He will say, "Mommy, I'm sorry."

3) Ask him to help clean it up. If the vase was expensive, there's not much you can do to get substantial compensation from a child who has no money, but you can let him know it was a favorite vase.

4) Say, "Since you and Bowser have so much energy, I think we need to figure out a way to get you outside and running around more often. Should we get a backyard swing set? Do you want to join the soccer league?"

5) Once the episode has been resolved, put it behind you. Do not mention it again. Don't use it as a club to beat him emotionally at a later date. (In a week, don't say, "You're always so clumsy! Just like the time you broke my favorite vase!")

Remember, even when you're upset and angry, if you want to help your child, steer them in a positive direction, and show them the way forward to being a happy, loving, self-sufficient, and engaged adult.

Children Model Their Parents

Research has shown that children really are like sponges. They soak up what they experience in the home, and make it a part of their own lives as they become adults.

In fact, the word researchers often use is "overimitation." This simply means that human children imitate the behavior and actions of their parents and caregivers so thoroughly that they imitate behaviors that can be considered irrelevant. In their report "Overimitation in Kalahari Bushman children and the origins of human cultural cognition," researchers M. Nielsen and K. Tomaselli from the University of Queensland in Australia wrote that from eighteen months of age, children will routinely copy even the arbitrary and unnecessary actions of their caregivers. The researchers documented similar behaviors exhibited by children from both a large, industrialized city and those from remote Bushman communities in southern Africa, thus revealing that overimitation may be a universal human trait. They concluded, "although seemingly maladaptive, overimitation reflects an evolutionary adaptation that is fundamental to the development and transmission of human culture."

Of course, this phenomenon applies primarily to young children who have not yet developed a strong sense of self. As the parent of any teenager knows, during adolescence the pendulum often swings the other way, and the child will strive mightily to do the *opposite* of what she sees the parent do. Any activity associated with the parent may become an anathema. If the dad has long hair, the son will get a buzz cut. If the mom enjoys attending the garden club, the daughter will be horrified at the idea of going to a garden club meeting.

This is a healthy stage. Your adolescent child needs to develop his or her own identity, be self-sufficient, and be able to get along with their peer group. If the family bonds are strong, the kids will eventually drift back. (Have you ever heard people in their thirties and forties say, "OMG, we're becoming our parents!" Yep, it really happens!)

Children pick up on the "vibes" their caregivers exude, whether positive or negative, confident or anxious. In their report "The Effect of Parental Modeling of Anxious Behaviors and Cognitions in School-Aged Children: An Experimental Pilot Study," researchers Marcy Burstein and Golda S. Ginsburg based their study on the accepted scientific knowledge that anxiety disorders aggregate within families and children of parents with anxiety disorders display higher rates of anxiety disorders than do relatives of family members without anxiety disorders. In a study in which carefully coached parents either expressed confidence or anxiety at the prospect of their child's performance in a spelling bee, they found that "regardless of parent gender, children endorsed higher anxiety levels, anxious cognitions, and desired avoidance of the spelling test in the anxious relative to the non-anxious condition."

In other words, your emotional response to any potential stressor, whether an upcoming spelling bee or broken vase, will be modeled by your child.

I'm sure you've seen this happen in ways both big and small.

If you shriek in horror when a spider strolls across your kitchen floor, your child will learn to shriek also.

If you see people of a different race and make nasty comments about them, your child will do the same.

If you fall and then get back up and say, "I'm okay—no problem!" your child will learn from you.

If you treat less fortunate people kindly, your child will express kindness too.

Chapter 5: Discipline

In the preceding chapter, we explored the importance of healthy parental responses to challenging situations and revealed how children take their behavioral cues from their caregivers.

Let's drill down into a related subject that for many parents can be contentious—the disciplining of your child, particularly with corporal punishment.

According to the American Academy of Pediatrics, "Corporal punishment involves the application of some form of physical pain in response to undesirable behavior," and "ranges from slapping the hand of a child about to touch a hot stove to identifiable child abuse, such as beatings, scaldings, and burnings. Because of this range in the form and severity of punishment, its use as a discipline strategy is controversial."

Today, the vast majority of child-care experts agree that no matter how egregious the transgression made by a child, inflicting physical punishment does no good, will only serve to make the child angry and resentful, and can twist their world view so that anger and even violence are acceptable to them.

This is a relatively modern concept.

For most of the history of mankind, corporal punishment was a routine practice, endorsed by civil and religious authorities. Beating one's child as a punishment was recommended as early as in the 10th century BCE, in the Book of Proverbs, attributed to Solomon. Here are just a few examples:

"He that spareth the rod, hateth his son; but he that loveth him, chasteneth him betimes." (Proverbs, XIII, 24)

"Chasten thy son while there is hope, and let not thy soul spare for his crying." (Proverbs, XIX, 18)

"Foolishness is bound in the heart of a child; but the rod of correction shall drive it from him." (Proverbs, XXII, 15)

"Withhold not correction from the child; for if thou beatest him with a rod, thou shalt deliver his soul from hell." (Proverbs, XXIII, 13–14)

If there was a logical justification for beating your child, I suppose it was because of the general lack of understanding of human psychology, and the belief that discipline was a simple cause and effect process: People don't like pain, so therefore if they receive pain for a crime, they will in the future avoid the crime and the pain. But now we know this naïve formulation is flat-out wrong. The human mind is far more complicated, and creating a culture of pain does more harm than good.

Some ancient experts disagreed with corporal punishment, at least for non-slaves; in the first century, Plutarch wrote in *The Education of Children*, a book contained within his *Moralia*:

"This also I assert, that children ought to be led to honorable practices by means of encouragement and reasoning, and most certainly not by blows or ill-treatment, for it surely is agreed that these are fitting rather for slaves than for the free-born; for so they grow numb and shudder at their tasks, partly from the pain of the blows, partly from the degradation."

By the way, perhaps thinking of future Tiger Moms everywhere, Plutarch also wrote, "In their eagerness that their children may the sooner rank first in everything, they lay upon them unreasonable tasks, which the children find themselves unable to perform, and so come to grief; besides, being depressed by their unfortunate experiences, they do not respond to the instruction which they receive." How true!

Perhaps as a reaction against the flagrant abuse of children working in factories during the Industrial Revolution, as well as the emergence of psychoanalysis, in the twentieth-century attitudes toward corporal punishment began to change. Today in the United States, corporal punishment of children in public schools and homes is a matter for the states to decide, and the current laws are a patchwork of inconsistency.

In public schools, according to "Corporal Punishment in U.S. Public Schools: Prevalence, Disparities in Use, and Status in State and Federal Policy" by Elizabeth T. Gershoff and Sarah A. Font, corporal punishment is currently legal in fifteen states, and over 106,000 children in these states are subject to corporal punishment in public schools each year. The approval of public school corporal punishment is heavily concentrated in Southern states: Alabama, Arkansas, Arizona, Florida, Georgia, Kansas, Kentucky, Louisiana,

Mississippi, Missouri, North Carolina, Oklahoma, South Carolina, Tennessee, Texas, and Wyoming. In the other thirty-one states, it's been outlawed in schools.

A typical state definition of school corporal punishment is the one offered in the Texas Education Code, which specifies permissible corporal punishment as, "the deliberate infliction of physical pain by hitting, paddling, spanking, slapping, or any other physical force used as a means of discipline." (Texas Education Code, 2013.)

Unfortunately, too often corporal punishment is not even used as a tool of last resort, such as against children who are violent. Gershoff and Font report that across various states, "children have been corporally punished in school for being late to class, failing to turn in homework, violating dress codes, running in the hallway, laughing in the hallway, sleeping in class, talking back to teachers, going to the bathroom without permission, mispronouncing words, and receiving bad grades."

Researchers have found that black students, boys, and disabled students continue to be physically punished at a greater rate than their classmates.

The pro-corporal punishment policies of these regressive states are contrary to the views of professional organizations. As Robert Kennedy wrote in 2019 for Thoughtco.com, the following organizations have stated their positions on corporal punishment:

The American Academy of Child and Adolescent Psychiatry "opposes the use of corporal punishment in schools and takes issue with laws in some states legalizing such corporal punishment and protecting adults who use it from prosecution for child abuse."

The American School Counselor Association: "ASCA seeks the elimination of corporal punishment in schools."

The American Academy of Pediatrics "recommends that corporal punishment in schools be abolished in all states by law and that alternative forms of student behavior management be used."

The National Association of Secondary School Principals "believes that the practice of corporal punishment in schools should be abolished and that principals should utilize alternative forms of discipline."

As a concerned parent, you should know that despite state laws that condone corporal punishment, your individual school district can formulate its own policy about corporal punishment, and even ban it or allow parents to opt-out. In North Carolina, for example, the last remaining school district to allow corporal punishment voted in October 2018 to ban the practice, effectively ending corporal punishment in the state, even though it's technically still permitted by state law. If your school district allows it, you can organize and put pressure on the school board to outlaw it.

If your child receives corporal punishment at school, and you are powerless to stop it, I recommend getting professional counseling.

Corporal Punishment at Home

In the United States, in your own home, corporal punishment is technically legal in all fifty states. Statutes vary from state to state, but generally say that the physical punishment must be "reasonable" or "not excessive." In 2012, Delaware passed a law that said it couldn't cause any injury or pain.

Sadly, corporal punishment in the home is still widespread. In their 2014 report "Eavesdropping on the family: a pilot investigation of corporal punishment in the home," researchers led by George W. Holden asked 33 mothers in Texas to wear digital audio recorders for up to six evenings. The results were startling. During the duration of the study, nearly half used some form of corporal punishment. They tended to use spanking not as a last resort but when they were angry and for trivial incidents, such as minor social transgressions by children. The researchers noted the episodes of corporal punishment were *not* usually effective in stopping unwanted behavior. According to lead author George Holden, "The recordings show that most parents responded either impulsively or emotionally, rather than being intentional with their discipline."

Make no mistake: Nearly every child care expert, doctor, and researcher say unequivocally that corporal punishment—generally meaning its most common form, spanking—is ineffective at best and damaging at worst.

After reviewing decades of research, Elizabeth Gershoff, PhD, a leading researcher on physical punishment at the University of Texas at Austin, wrote in "Report on Physical Punishment in the United States: What Research Tells Us About Its Effects on Children," published in 2008 in conjunction with Phoenix Children's Hospital, that parents and caregivers should make every effort to avoid physical punishment, and called for the banning of physical discipline in all U.S. schools. The report has been endorsed by dozens of organizations, including the American Academy of Pediatrics, American Medical Association, and Psychologists for Social Responsibility.

The report states that aside from being ineffective as a way to improve behavior, "physical punishment makes it more likely that children will be defiant and aggressive in the future; physical punishment puts children at risk for negative outcomes, including increased mental health problems; and children who are physically punished are at a greater risk of serious injury and physical abuse."

The Way Forward

If we accept the idea that physical punishment is both ineffective and damaging, what's the harried parent to do when Johnny or Suzy throws a tantrum, or screams "Drop dead!" at mommy, or throws their bowl of peas against the wall?

Here's one viewpoint. The Parent Management Training program headed by Alan Kazdin, PhD, a Yale University psychology professor and director of the Yale Parenting Center and Child Conduct Clinic, teaches a technique that may sound crazy to most parents: Telling toddlers to *practice* throwing a tantrum. Just ask your child to have a pretend tantrum minus the undesirable element, such as hitting or kicking. Let them scream and roll around on the floor. Kazdin says that as children practice controlling tantrums when they aren't angry, their real tantrums are less violent.

During a child's tantrum, it's important for you—the caregiver—to remain calm. *Do not allow your child to control your behavior!* Don't give the wild child the satisfaction of an audience. When the fury has subsided, say, "Do you feel better now? Are you ready to talk about what you want?" You should talk with your child about appropriate means of resolving conflicts. Building a trusting relationship can help children believe that discipline isn't arbitrary or done out of anger.

The American Psychological Association (APA) offers the Adults & Children Together Against Violence program, which provides parenting skills classes through a nationwide research-based program called Parents Raising Safe Kids. The course teaches parents how to avoid violence through anger management, positive child discipline, and conflict resolution.

Carl Ransom Rogers, a 20th-century American psychologist, was among the founders of the humanistic approach (or client-centered approach) to psychology. In 1951 he published a wide-ranging book entitled *Client-Centered Therapy*, which addressed, among other topics, the education of children. Among his five hypotheses regarding learner-centered education, he wrote:

"The structure and organization of self appears to become more rigid under threats, and to relax its boundaries when completely free from threat," and,

"The educational situation which most effectively promotes significant learning is one in which a threat to the self of the learner is reduced to a minimum…"

Going back to your overall goal as a parent, which is to raise your child to become an adult who is happy, loving, self-sufficient, and engaged in life, the strategy of teaching the child the positive way to live is far more effective than using fear or pain to avoid bad behavior, because with the punitive approach, even if the child figures out what behavior is bad, he or she will have no clue about what behavior is good.

Imagine a traveler comes to you and asks for directions. The traveler says, "I'm trying to get to the Emerald City. Which way should I go?"

And you answer, "Do not go across the river. Do not go through the forest. Do not go by the lake."

The traveler is rightly mystified. "Excuse me," he says, "You've told me some ways I must not go. That information doesn't help me. Which way *should* I go?"

Then you answer, "Oh, sorry. It's easy. Follow the yellow brick road. It will take you there."

So, if providing valuable life information to your child is the goal, it's important to know that, as Rogers astutely pointed out, people are far more receptive to learning when they feel comfortable and not threatened. When people, including children, feel emotionally or physically assailed, their immediate, reflexive response is to become emotionally and intellectually rigid and resist the influence of the attacker. This is because they feel their sense of self-being threatened. They do not want to assimilate the lesson being pushed upon them because they believe it will alter their very essence. But when they feel secure in their sense of self, they are open to new ideas, even ones that might require a change of behavior.

At some point, every parent will put their foot down and shout "Enough!" If you do this, don't beat yourself up. You are human. You will make mistakes. To keep such parental outbursts to a minimum, follow these powerful tips:

- **Stay consistent.** Try not to respond emotionally to your children's behavior. Your child will be mystified if one exuberant outburst is applauded while the next one is condemned. Kids need to know the boundaries, and they need to know that while the law may bend, it's not going to break.

- **Use positive reinforcement.** Instead of just punishing them for what's bad, when your children behave appropriately be sure to praise them. In fact, it's more important to reward good behavior than to criticize the negative. Remember the example of the yellow brick road: Always show them the way to becoming happy, loving, self-sufficient, and engaged in life.

- **Try timeouts.** Effective discipline is nuanced, and not every strategy will work for every child. However, timeouts work for many families. As you're disciplining your child, specify the negative behavior, so he understands why he's being punished. Say, "You didn't stop jumping on the sofa, so you're going to your room for a timeout." Link the punishment to the offense, and do it quickly and clearly.

  If possible, do not send your child to their bedroom for a timeout, because it's probably a fun place to be, with toys and other distractions. Send them somewhere boring. Do not send them to a scary place, like a closet. That's tantamount to child abuse.

  At the end of the allotted time (experts recommend one minute per year of age), explain again to your child what they did wrong, ask for an apology, and give them a hug. Forgive and forget. Be careful because some children use timeouts as a way of getting extra attention. If you sense this is happening, try one of the other methods.

- **Redirect behavior.** Say, "You can't jump on the couch, but you can jump outside in the yard." Give the child a better choice than what they're doing now.

- **Take a break.** If you're feeling like you're "at your wit's end," put your child in a safe place and retreat for a few minutes. Say, "Mommy is really upset right now, and I need to take a few minutes to calm down. You stay here and play. I'll be back."

Toddlers and Young Children: A Reality Check

Having read this chapter, if you have a toddler or young child, you may be thinking, "Are we supposed to explain every little decision to our child? When we say 'don't run in the house,' do we have to provide a detailed reason why we don't want our child to zoom around the living room like a human rocket? I don't have time for that!"

You are absolutely right. Anyone who has been a parent knows that in the early ambulatory years, when you simply have to get your child from point A to point B without injury or delay, or when you're trying to get dinner on the table, or when it's bath time, you spend most of your time issuing commands, most of which include the word "don't":

"Suzy, don't pull the cat's tail."

"Jimmy, don't throw your spoon on the floor."

"Rachel, don't jump on the sofa."

"Khalid, don't use your toy truck as a hammer."

Sometimes it feels like your life is nothing but an endless stream of "don'ts." It's balanced only by the equally endless stream of "do's":

"Suzy, brush your teeth."

"Jimmy, eat your peas."

"Rachel, put on your coat."

"Khalid, go to sleep."

This is reality, and there's nothing wrong with it. Think of these "do's" and "don'ts" as minute-by-minute course corrections as if you were steering a sailboat across the wide lake to your destination. It's just something you do without much analysis.

Limiting your child's actions by saying "don't" is perfectly fine as long as *two conditions are met:*

1. If your child *generally* feels they have control and authority over their own actions, they won't feel resentful or threatened when you say "no" to some *particular* action. They'll just change course and do something else. So, if Suzy is pulling the cat's tail and you say, "Please stop," then if pulling the cat's tail is not particularly important to her because there are other things she can do on her own, she won't care if the cat option is taken away. It's not necessary that you suggest some other activity, but it can help. So, therefore, you might say, "Suzy, please don't pull the cat's tail. Why don't you read your new book, or help mommy make the bed?"

2. Choose your battles. Don't say "don't" over and over again for no good reason. I'm sure you've seen parents who, when they're with their child, endlessly say "don't do this" and "don't do that," even though the child isn't really doing anything dangerous or objectionable. Then you look at the child, and of course, they aren't paying any attention to the nonsense coming from the parent's mouth. Who would? The child learns to ignore the parent who says "don't," until the parent gets *really* mad and threatens to smack them. Obviously, this is not a healthy situation.

Always remember the goal: You want your child to become an adult who is happy, loving, self-sufficient, and engaged in life. This means a child who has enough autonomy so that when you say "no," it really means something, and the child will willingly comply.

Chapter 6: Attachment and Exploration

I'm sure you've seen those parents who have their child glued to them. If the child is a baby, he or she will be confined in one of those papoose devices that hold the infant tightly against the parent's body. The parent keeps their infant close and doesn't want their precious darling to experience the cruel vagaries of the outside world.

When the toddler is old enough to walk on their own, he or she clings to the parent's leg or plants itself on the parent's lap. The toddler's face wears an expression of anxiety.

The next stage is the fearful child who's incapable of entering new situations or meeting new people. On the first day of school, the excessively sheltered child will cry and resist getting on the school bus or walking into the front door of the big, scary school. He or she will not make friends easily, and thus the negativity of the school experience becomes a self-fulfilling prophecy. The child expects to be ostracized, and by expecting it, makes it happen.

On the other hand, I'm sure you've seen those parents who let their child do anything they want, whenever they want. They say they don't want their kid to have boundaries. They let the child stay up as long as he or she wants and doesn't set firm curfews. These are often the parents who ship their kids off to summer camp as soon as they're old enough to feed themselves, and then when they get a little older send them to boarding school. You can get the feeling the parents just aren't that interested in exercising hands-on guidance of their child. They toss their child into the raging sea of life, to sink or swim.

These are the extremes of attachment and exploration. As is so often the case with child-rearing, the best path is the one right down the middle, the happy medium. In the proper measure, both attachment and exploration are vital to human development, each in their own way.

As Mary D. Salter Ainsworth and Silvia M. Bell wrote in "Attachment, exploration, and separation: Illustrated by the behavior of one-year-olds in a strange situation" (1970), an "attachment" may be defined as "an affectional tie that one person or animal forms between himself and another specific one—a tie that binds them together in space and endures over time." The person(s) seeking the attachment (it may be both parent and child) will engage in close physical contact whenever possible. In children, these include signaling behaviors such as smiling, crying, and calling, as well as active proximity- and contact-seeking behaviors including approaching, following, and clinging.

The impulse for attachment is strong and has a clear biological function. In particular, the infant-mother attachment may be seen to promote species survival. As the authors write, "The long, helpless infancy of the human species occasions grave risks. For the species to have survived, the infant has required protection during this period of defenselessness. It is inferred, therefore, that the genetic code makes provision for infant behaviors which have the usual (although not necessarily invariable) outcome of bringing infant and mother together." In other words, the forming of a strong mother-infant attachment may be hard-wired into our DNA; presumably, humans who were not genetically programmed to form this attachment would be more likely to perish, and with them, their non-attachment DNA.

From the point of view of evolution, exploratory behavior is equally significant. An infant would not develop fully if there were not also aspects of his or her genetic code that encouraged them to be curious about the novel features of their environment—to venture forth, to explore, and to learn.

As humans go through life, we need to adapt to a wide range of environmental conditions. This requires a balance in both infant and maternal behaviors between those which lead the infant away from the mother, promoting exploration and acquisition of knowledge of the outside world, and those which draw mother and infant together, promoting the protection and nurturance that the mother can provide.

Ainsworth's "Strange Situation"

The "Strange Situation" is a procedure devised by developmental psychologist Mary Ainsworth in the 1970s to observe attachment relationships between the caregiver (for simplicity, we'll say parent) and child. It applies to children between the age of nine and eighteen months. In her test, each child was observed playing for twenty-one minutes while the parent and strangers entered and left the room, creating a flow of the familiar and unfamiliar, while responses were observed. The approach of the stranger was gradual so that any fear of her could be attributed to unfamiliarity rather than abrupt, alarming behavior.

The Strange Situation procedure provided a good opportunity to observe how exploratory behavior was affected by parent-present, parent-absent, or other conditions. During each test period, the researchers observed the child's behaviors and assigned those behaviors into various categories including exploratory behavior, crying, search behavior during separation, proximity-seeking and contact-maintaining behaviors, and contact-resisting and proximity-avoiding behaviors.

Based on the sum total of these behaviors, Ainsworth placed each child within one of three categories, with a fourth category added later. The categories are:

1. Secure

While the parent is present, this child will explore and play freely, using her as a "secure base" from which to investigate its surroundings. When the parent is present, the child will engage with the stranger. While the child may be visibly upset when the parent departs, she's happy to see the parent on his or her return.

Securely attached children are best able to explore when they have the knowledge of a secure base to return to in times of need. When assistance is given, this bolsters the sense of security and also, assuming the parent's assistance is helpful, educates the child on how to cope with the same problem in the future.

2. Anxious-avoidant, insecure

This infant will avoid or ignore the caregiver, showing little emotion when the caregiver departs or returns. The child will not explore very much regardless of who is there. Appropriate characterizations might be indifference or lack of awareness. Ainsworth and Bell theorized that the apparently detached behavior of the avoidant infants was, in fact, a mask for distress, a hypothesis later evidenced through studies of the heart rate of avoidant infants.

From whence does such behavior come? It's actually rather simple: the parent has trained the child to believe the parent is undependable and even irrelevant. The parent has done this by ignoring the child's pleas for attention or help, and consequently, the child learns that communication of needs has no influence on the parent.

Ainsworth's student Mary Main proposed that avoidance has two practical functions for an infant whose caregiver is consistently unresponsive to their needs.

Firstly, avoidant behavior allows the infant to maintain a *conditional proximity* with the caregiver: close enough to benefit from the parent's protection, but far enough away to avoid rebuff.

Secondly, the cognitive processes required for avoidant behavior could help distract the child from her unfulfilled desire for closeness with the parent—that is, to help the child rationalize and accept a stressful situation.

As a parent, what this means for you is this: *you're going to get the relationship you create with your child.* If you keep your child at arm's length, don't expect your child to develop a strong, loving bond with you. You didn't want a loving bond, so you're not going to get it. But if you want a strong and loving bond, and you practice it every day, the odds are in your favor that when your child becomes an adult, that's the relationship you'll have.

3. Anxious-ambivalent/resistant, insecure

Children classified as anxious-ambivalent/resistant show distress even before separation, and are clingy and difficult to comfort on the parent's return. In response to the parent's absence, they show signs of either 1) resentment or 2) helpless passivity.

Researchers believe the anxious-ambivalent/resistant strategy is a response to unpredictable caregiving, and that the displays of either anger or helplessness towards the caregiver on reunion are a strategy to maintain the availability of the caregiver by preemptively taking control of the interaction.

In other words, unlike the detached, unconcerned avoidant child who ignores the parent, the resistant/insecure child seeks to get the parent's attention, but can only do this in a *negative* way, by generating either anger or sympathy from the parent, not genuine love and caring.

4. Disorganized/disoriented

This fourth classification was suggested by Mary Main. In the Strange Situation, the child's response is expected to be activated by the departure and return of the parent. But if the infant's response does not appear to achieve some relative proximity with the caregiver, then it is considered "disorganized," as it indicates a disruption or "flooding" of the attachment system by some emotion such as fear. Infant behaviors coded as disorganized/disoriented include overt displays of fear; contradictory behaviors or affects occurring simultaneously or sequentially; stereotypic, asymmetric, misdirected or jerky movements; or freezing and apparent dissociation.

Sometimes these are initial symptoms that, within a short period of time, resolve themselves into one of the other classifications. Tellingly, subsequent researchers found that most of the mothers of these disorganized/disoriented children had suffered major losses or other trauma shortly before or after the birth of the infant and had reacted by becoming severely depressed. Many mothers who had lost a parent by death before they completed high school subsequently had children with disorganized attachments.

Reactive Attachment Disorder (RAD)

The bond formed between parent and child from infancy has been shown to be critically important as the child moves through adolescence and beyond.

Reactive attachment disorder is characterized by a child's markedly disturbed and developmentally inappropriate ways of relating socially. It can take the form of a persistent failure to initiate or respond to most social interactions in a developmentally appropriate way. This is known as the "inhibited form."

What causes RAD? It begins in early childhood from a lack of healthy attachments to primary caregivers. This can result from severe early experiences of abuse, neglect, frequent change of caregivers, abrupt separation from caregivers in infancy, or a lack of caregiver responsiveness to a child's communicative efforts. In a sense, it's a psychological form of an adverse childhood experience, which we discussed earlier in the book. And, as we learned, such experiences can lead to long-lasting alterations of hormones and even genetic expression.

According to the "Report of the APSAC Task Force on Attachment Therapy, Reactive Attachment Disorder, and Attachment Problems" (2006) by Mark Chaffin and colleagues, the core feature of RAD is severely inappropriate social relating by affected children. This can manifest itself in three ways:

1. Indiscriminate and excessive attempts to receive comfort and affection from any available adult, even relative strangers. Older children and adolescents may also aim attempts at peers. This may oftentimes appear as the reverse—denial of comfort from anyone as well.

2. Extreme reluctance to initiate or accept comfort and affection, even from familiar adults, especially when distressed.

3. Actions that otherwise would be classified as conduct disorder, such as mutilating animals, harming siblings or other family, or harming themselves intentionally.

Without delving too exhaustively into everything that can go wrong in the attachment between parent and child, suffice to say that what you do as a parent *matters*. It makes a difference to your child. This does not mean that you need to be paranoid or constantly second-guessing yourself. Conceptually, being a good parent and forming a close attachment to your child is easy.

All you have to do is treat your child the way you would want to be treated.

When your child falls, help them get up again.
When your child succeeds, praise them.
When your child needs love, hug them.
It's really pretty simple!

Piaget and the Importance of Exploration

For a child, "exploration" means learning about the world around them in a way that is safe and incremental.

The idea that children explore in stages corresponding to their age was first proposed by the early 20th-century Swiss psychologist Jean Piaget, who was known for his work on child development. Piaget's theory of cognitive development explained how a child constructs a mental model of the world. An important feature of his theory was the assertion that intelligence is *not* a fixed trait; instead, cognitive development is a *process* involving biological maturation and interaction with the environment. In other words, intelligence is as much nurture as nature and can be influenced by the parents.

Instead of being passive, empty vessels, needing to be filled by teachers or parents, Piaget believed children take an active role in the learning process, acting much like budding scientists as they make observations, perform experiments, and learn about the world. As kids interact with the world around them, they continually build upon existing knowledge, add new knowledge, and modify previously held ideas to accommodate new information.

In fact, Piaget concluded that children were not less intelligent than adults; they simply had different thought processes. Albert Einstein called Piaget's discovery "so simple only a genius could have thought of it."

When you think about that, it makes sense, particularly in regard to the *rate of learning*. Consider a normal child's development from birth to age two. It's astonishing how much a child learns in just two short years—from knowing literally nothing and having extremely limited motor skills to being able to walk, talk, relate to other people and understand abstract concepts like something being funny or scary. Ask yourself—how much have you learned in the past two years? Not as much as your child!

Piaget's theory of cognitive development suggests that children move through four different stages of mental development. Piaget's stages are:

1. Sensorimotor stage: birth to two years

Infants learn about the world through basic actions such as sucking, grasping, looking, and listening. They realize their actions can affect the world around them. They go through a period of dramatic growth and learning, and as they interact with their environment, they are continually making new discoveries about how the world works, including how to interact with the big hairy people who provide love, food, and protection. They learn the names of the various people in their lives, and if they can't pronounce someone's name, they will invent one.

They learn a great deal about language from the people with whom they interact, and they develop the concept of object permanence or object constancy, which is the understanding that objects and people continue to exist even when they cannot be seen. As a parent, one of the most important things you can do—aside from being a nice, loving person—is to be dependable and consistent. Don't get tangled up in theory. Treat your baby like someone who will eventually become a rational, self-sufficient person, but who has a lot to learn along the way.

2. Preoperational stage: ages two to seven

Language development is one of the hallmarks of this period. Children begin to think symbolically and learn to use words and pictures to represent objects.

While children continue to think very concretely about the world around them, they become much more skilled at pretend play. For example, a child is able to use an object to represent something else, such as pretending a cardboard box is a boat. Role-playing also becomes important, with children playing the roles of "mommy," "daddy," "doctor," and other characters.

Despite this role-playing ability, as any parent knows, children tend to be egocentric and have difficulty seeing a situation from the perspective of another. Developmental psychologists refer to the ability to understand that other people have different perspectives, thoughts, feelings, and mental states as a theory of mind—and kids at this age may not be there yet.

Be patient with your child's thoughtlessness, and reward those moments representing progress towards the goal of becoming an adult who is happy, loving, self-sufficient, and engaged in life.

3. Concrete operational stage: ages seven to eleven

Spanning the time of middle childhood, it's characterized by the development of logical thought. Piaget determined that children in the concrete operational stage were fairly good at the use of inductive logic (inductive reasoning). Inductive logic involves going from a specific experience to a general principle.

An example of inductive logic would be noticing that big kids ride two-wheel bikes, while little kids ride tricycles. Therefore, riding a two-wheel bike means you must be a big kid.

There is a danger to this type of reasoning that you, as a parent, need to guard against. For example, if your daughter sees that most astronauts are men, and therefore concludes that women are not astronauts, this is a limiting belief based not on human capability but on an inaccurate preconception that can be changed.

Similarly, if the child's father is an alcoholic, it's easy for the child to grow up believing that fathers tend to be alcoholics. If the child's mother abandons the child, the child may grow up assuming this is what mothers do. Sadly, we see this familial effect in suicide statistics. According to the National Institute of Mental Health, a family history of suicide and mental or substance abuse disorder are among the most prevalent risk factors for suicide in the United

States. Although only a small proportion of people have such a family history, parents should be aware of its strong influence and should be attentive to relevant signs while dealing with suicidal people, particularly adolescents and young adults. As the US Department of Health and Human Services has said, "Suicide contagion is the exposure to suicide or suicidal behaviors within one's family, one's peer group, or through media reports of suicide, and can result in an increase in suicide and suicidal behaviors. Direct and indirect exposure to suicidal behavior has been shown to precede an increase in suicidal behavior in persons at risk for suicide, especially in adolescents and young adults."

Thankfully, the concrete operational stage is also characterized by decreases in egocentrism. While children in the preoperational stage struggle to understand the perspective of others, kids in the concrete stage are able to think about things the way that others see them.

4. Formal operational stage: ages twelve and up

At this stage, the adolescent begins to think abstractly and reason about hypothetical problems. They begin to think more about moral, philosophical, ethical, social, and political issues that require theoretical and abstract reasoning.

Kids are now capable of answering "What if...?" questions that may appear to be contrary to fact. For example, you could ask, "What if dolphins could speak English?" A younger child might think such an idea to be funny and absurd, while the twelve-year-old might respond, "Gee, I wonder what that would be like?" Thinking more scientifically about the world around them, they become capable of seeing multiple potential solutions to problems. The abilities to systematically plan for the future and reason about hypothetical situations are also critical abilities that emerge during this stage.

One practical effect of this development is that your kids become aware of, and affected by, what they see in other people's families and households. They can imagine what their single-parent household would be like with two parents, or if they had a parent who let their child eat junk food and watch TV all day. This coincides with the emerging desire to identify with and have the approval of, their peer group. Is the solution, therefore, to restrict your child or shield them from outside influences that may challenge their parochial worldview? (At the far extreme, this is what cults do. They prohibit contact with the outside world.) Or is it better to let them see a broad horizon, knowing that in the first twelve or fourteen years of their life you've instilled in them values that will serve as a strong anchor?

Play Is Exploration

From the day a child is born, he or she is bombarded with a ceaseless flood of stimuli and information. The physical world, human relationships, eating, sleeping, danger, safety, language—so much to learn. And yet most kids, when left to their own devices, instead of being burned out on learning overload, will eagerly set about learning more—by playing.

"It's hard to imagine when an infant or a toddler *isn't* playing," said Catherine Tamis-LeMonda, a professor of applied psychology at New York University who studies play and learning in babies and young children, to *The New York Times*. She cited, for example, the joys of smooshing your food, pulling books off a shelf, or making noises rattling a paper bag.

"I don't like it when scientists think children are playing only when they sit down with some toys," she told reporter Perri Klass, MD. "Almost all the learning that goes on in the first years of life is in the context of exploration of the environment."

She conducts her research by going into people's homes and watching their kids play. "We think that all domains of development are informed by children engaging in play," she said. Babies and kids learn as they play—getting motor practice as they climb, crawl, and run; learning words and concepts as they engage with objects in their environment, and; even developing spatial math concepts when they pull the books off a shelf. They re-enact their own experiences by pretending to care for their dolls and gain social development by learning to take turns.

Regrettably, as children are immersed in a school environment, free play is often suppressed by the relentless pursuit of goals. But free play reduces stress and allows kids to free-associate for themselves. Children love to engage with real objects, handling them, building with them, dropping them, and throwing them. Screen time digital "play" is a poor substitute for actually moving through space, interacting with their environment, and building whole-body coordination and fitness.

As protective parents, it's tempting to want to create an environment free of risk. But this is shortsighted. As researchers, Gabriela Bento and Gisela Dias wrote in "The importance of outdoor play for young children's healthy development," our culture often neglects the importance of risk for children's learning and development. A culture of fear—of strangers, accidents, disease from nasty germs—has led us to underestimate what children are capable of doing, which creates, as they wrote, "an even more 'dangerous' learning environment, where children do not have the possibility to learn, by experience, *how* to stay safe. It is essential to adopt a wider vision of risk, going beyond the possibility of accidents to consider the positive implications related to the feelings of success and happiness when a challenge or a new skill is mastered."

Attachment and exploration are two sides of the same coin, and every parent should strive to provide both.

Chapter 7: Empathy

Most parents with young children look for those rewarding moments when they see evidence of their child's growing maturity. One such moment may come when their child shows empathy for another person or an animal—when little Suzy offers to share her cookie with a classmate who has none, or when Billy sees a baby bird on the ground and asks mommy if they can help it to fly.

Empathy is the ability to understand and respond to the feelings of others. It is at the root of a child's ability to be kind and compassionate.

But let's ask ourselves: what good is empathy? Why should human beings value it?

After all, in a dog-eat-dog world where each individual competed to survive, empathy would be a liability and a sign of weakness. There would be no reason to help another because life would be a zero-sum game: I win and you lose. In such a world, if your opponent is down, your job is not to help him to his feet but to crush him and take his treasure.

But if that were how human beings operated millions of years ago, we would never have survived as a species. Individually, we are ill-suited for survival and reproduction. We have no natural weapons, we don't run very fast, and our infants require years of careful upbringing before they can fend for themselves. We've been able to survive and thrive only because we've bonded together into social units: tribes, communities, nations. We've learned to subsume the interests of the individual into those of the community. One of the traits that have helped bind us together is empathy, or the ability and willingness to recognize when one of our members is in distress and to respond altruistically, thus benefitting the community as a whole.

As parents, we look for those first signs of empathy in our children. But as all parents know, empathy isn't like a light switch that's turned on once and then stays on forever. In most kids, it seems to surface in fits and starts. Little Billy might cradle an injured bunny one day, and the next day goes outside with a magnifying glass and gleefully fry ants under the hot sun. That's emblematic of the understandable push and pull between being willing to sacrifice for others, while, on the other hand, thinking only of our own survival and pleasure.

As Erin Walsh, M.A. and David Walsh, Ph.D. noted in their article, "How Children Develop Empathy," it evolves throughout childhood and adolescence. In general, a child can be said to have empathy when he or she:

• Understands they are a distinct person from those around them, and that other people may have different feelings and viewpoints than their own

• Can recognize feelings in themselves and others, and can name them

- Can identify and regulate their own emotional responses
- Can see the world from someone else's perspective and imagine how they might be feeling
- Can imagine the action or response that could help a person feel better
- Is willing to put the feelings of another person before their own

Empathy does not simply unfold automatically in children. It's shaped by a multitude of forces including environment, genetics, temperament, and context. While the vast majority of humans are born hardwired with the capacity for empathy, its development requires deliberate nurturing.

Keep in mind that if you believe humans must depend upon each other for survival, then empathy can be seen as self-serving because the bottom line is that the subject (the person who empathizes) hopes to indirectly benefit from helping ease the pain of the object (the person who is suffering). This can be seen most blatantly in the scenario of a child who sees their mother is sick or incapacitated and seeks to help the mother get better so the mother can get back to doing what mothers do, which is care for their children. In its most grotesque manifestation, this is like the story of the pet dog who sees its owner has died, and expresses great grief and tries to revive the owner. Eventually, as hunger sets in and the beloved owner is not responding, the pet dog starts to eat the owner.

Setting aside these shades of interpretation, just about everyone agrees that human empathy is a good thing, and its development should be encouraged in children.

Empathy exists in both emotional and cognitive realms.

In children, the emotional aspects of empathy are the first to emerge. As soon as they are aware of their surroundings, babies begin reflecting on the emotional states and expressions of those around them. In the brain, "mirror neurons" are those that fire both when a person acts and when the person observes the same action performed by another. Thus, the neuron "mirrors" the behavior of the other, as though the observer were itself acting.

Such neurons have been directly observed in primate species, including humans as young as a day old, who can show some responsiveness to other infants in distress. No one teaches babies how to do this; they are born hardwired to map the experiences of others in their brains and bodies.

But babies are also hardwired to get what they want for themselves. When they're hungry, they cry for attention. They may be suspicious or jealous of other children, or new children, who seem to enjoy the favor of the parent. Children may take from others just because they want what the other child has. Adolescents may steal money from their parent's purse. While we humans have a strong inclination to help others, we have an equally strong desire to help ourselves.

This tug of war between egoism and altruism takes place in the brain.

In a study published in The Journal of Neuroscience in October 2013, a research team headed by Tania Singer from the Max Planck Institute for Human Cognitive and Brain Sciences identified that while the tendency to be egocentric is innate for human beings, a part of your brain recognizes a lack of empathy and autocorrects. In "I'm ok, you're not ok: The right supramarginal gyrus plays an important role in empathy," they revealed this specific part of the brain is called the right supramarginal gyrus. It's located at the junction of the parietal, temporal, and frontal lobe.

The experiment was very simple. Participants were divided into pairs. Both were presented with stimuli—images and sensations. Sometimes the stimuli were pleasant, while at other times the stimuli were disturbing. Then each participant was asked about the other person's feelings. The researchers found that if both participants were exposed to the same type of either positive or negative stimuli, they found it easy to assess their partner's emotions. The participant who was confronted with a spider, and who felt alarmed, could easily imagine how similarly alarming the sight of a spider was for her partner.

But during the test runs in which one partner was confronted with pleasant stimuli and the other with something unpleasant, the participants' capacity for empathy suddenly evaporated. As the researcher wrote, "The participants' own emotions distorted their assessment of the other person's feelings. The participants who were feeling good themselves assessed their partners' negative experiences as less severe than they were. In contrast, those who had just had an unpleasant experience assessed their partners' good experiences less positively."

In other words, when it comes to empathy, we instinctively respond to others who are having an experience that is familiar and tangible to us. If their experience contradicts our own, we have more difficulty, and a conscious effort is required.

With the help of functional magnetic resonance imaging, or brain scanning, the researchers revealed the area of the brain responsible for this phenomenon. The right supramarginal gyrus enables us to "decouple" our perception of ourselves from that of others. That means it helps us to set aside our own feelings and be objective. It helps us to feel empathy for someone who has been handed a spider when no such creature has been shown to us.

The researchers discovered "when the neurons in this part of the brain were disrupted in the course of this task, the participants found it difficult not to project their own feelings onto others. The participants' assessments were also less accurate when they were forced to make particularly quick decisions."

The results showed that when gathering information about the emotional state of others, we use our own feelings as a template and tend to project our own emotional state onto others. The researchers called it "emotional egocentricity," which the right supramarginal gyrus can override, allowing for greater objectivity.

Some people have difficulty feeling any empathy.

Psychopathy is a personality disorder characterized by "a lack of empathy and remorse, shallow affect, glibness, manipulation, and callousness." People with the disorder have limited aversive arousal to the distress and sadness cues of others.

When individuals with psychopathy are exposed to information about others feeling pain, researchers have found that the brain areas necessary for feeling empathy fail to become active, and are not connected to other regions responsible for affective processing and compassionate decision-making.

To make it worse, as Jean Decety and colleagues wrote in their 2013 article, "An FMRI study of affective perspective taking in individuals with psychopathy: imagining another in pain does not evoke empathy," when highly psychopathic participants imagined pain inflicted upon themselves, they showed a standard neural response within those brain regions involved in empathy for pain, including the anterior insula, the anterior midcingulate cortex, somatosensory cortex, and the right amygdala. In fact, the increase in brain activity in these regions was unusually pronounced, suggesting that psychopathic people are sensitive to the thought of their own pain.

But when the same participants imagined pain inflicted upon others, in those who were considered "high psychopaths," these regions failed to become active. In fact, when imagining others in pain, psychopaths actually showed an increased response in the ventral striatum, an area known to be involved in pleasure.

What this means is that barring a serious mental disease, all human beings have the brain equipment to feel empathy and to decouple their own feelings from the feelings perceived in others. Because our brain's neural circuitry is malleable and can be rewired through neuroplasticity, our capacity for empathy and compassion can be modified. Empathy can, and should, be developed; and parents are in the best position to do this so that children can learn to "love thy neighbor as thyself" and "do unto others as you would have them do unto you."

Bullying

In recent years, increased attention has been paid to the problem of bullying among children and teenagers.

In 2014, the Centers for Disease Control and Department of Education released the first federal uniform definition of bullying for research and surveillance. The core elements of the definition include: unwanted aggressive behavior; observed or perceived power imbalance; and repetition of behaviors or high likelihood of repetition.

According to StopBullying.gov, the most common types of bullying are verbal and social. As many as 30 percent of U.S. students say they have been bullied at school, most often in middle school. Roughly 15 percent have experienced cyberbullying. Other sources put the number even higher—the i-SAFE foundation states that over "25 percent of adolescents and teens have been bullied repeatedly through their cell phones or the Internet."

There are many different modes and types of bullying.

The current definition acknowledges two modes and four types by which youth can be bullied or can bully others. The two modes of bullying include direct (e.g., bullying that occurs in the presence of a targeted youth) and indirect (e.g., bullying not directly communicated to a targeted youth, such as spreading rumors). In addition to these two modes, the four types of bullying include broad categories of physical, verbal, relational (e.g., efforts to harm the reputation or relationships of the targeted youth), and damage to property.

Bullying tends to happen in public—that is to say, the bully derives emotional satisfaction from knowing that his or her peer group has witnessed the attack, and presumably approves. This is where the development of empathy in a child can be so important. StopBullying.gov reports that:

• 70.6 percent of young people say they have seen bullying in their schools.

• When bystanders intervene, in 57 percent of cases the bullying stops within 10 seconds.

This means that not only does a well-developed sense of empathy help prevent a child from becoming a bully, it can also help the child provide support and encouragement to another child who is being bullied, thereby blunting the effect of the attack and discouraging future attacks.

Empathy—the enemy of bullying—can be learned. As Dr. Patty O'Grady wrote in *Positive Psychology in the Elementary School Classroom,* "Kindness changes the brain by the experience of kindness. Children and adolescents do not learn kindness by only thinking about it and talking about it. Kindness is best learned by feeling it so that they can reproduce it."

Stages and Steps

Here are some of the stages of empathy development and the steps you can take to help your child develop this important character trait.

Age Zero to Two

Possessed by an innate compulsion to ingratiate themselves with their big hairy masters on the strange planet, infants are keenly aware of the emotional responses of the people around them and seek to mimic their behavior.

Ten-month-old Keesha loves to put the blanket on her head, pull it off, and then look at her parents for smiles of approval. With this simple game, she's learning to read facial and verbal cues, and how to repeat behaviors that make people laugh. She is becoming aware of the various people in her orbit and how they are feeling, which can be an essential precursor to empathy.

I say "can be" a precursor because while infants and toddlers are sensitive to the "vibes" in the room, they don't yet feel empathy. Let's say that Randy, who is one year old, begins to cry when his mother is temporarily out of sight. His playmate Sylvie, of the same age, is next to him. She stops playing and looks at Randy. While Randy's tears may have triggered a feeling of anxiety in Sylvie, she's not aware of the reason he's crying, and knows not to comfort him.

If Randy's mother comes back and picks him up and comforts him with soothing words, Sylvie will see this and subconsciously file it away in her mind as being the appropriate response. Likewise, if Randy's mother returns and says in a sharp voice, "Why are you crying? If you don't stop right now, we're leaving. Do you hear me?" Sylvie may be disturbed by her tone and learn that crying equals getting yelled at.

At such an early age, the best thing you can do is set a good example in how you treat your child, other children, family pets—indeed, any living thing that you encounter during the day. Show your child the joy that comes from being with other people and in nature. Express happiness when your toddler shares or voluntarily give their playmate a hug. But keep your expectations low. Infants and toddlers are in a precarious position in life, and they can be forgiven if they are programmed to pursue only their own survival.

The lesson they can learn, though, is that their survival is much more certain and more pleasant if they get along with others, which means being in tune with what others are feeling.

Three and Four

Having become both ambulatory and verbal, kids at this age are more skilled at imitating acceptable behavior and currying favor with their parents. They are learning about cause and effect. They understand, for example, that Bowser, the pet dog, can become hungry, and if you feed him, he will become happy. They can comprehend that if a playmate falls and cuts their knee, it's painful, and the playmate will need extra hugs and kisses. But they may not grasp what these things they see really mean, and they need a caregiver's guidance to connect the dots.

Here are some ways you can help young children learn to be more empathic and understand how other people express their feelings:

Teach words about feelings and emotions. When your child is distressed, ask them what would make them feel better. Ask, "Are you sad? Does your tummy hurt? Do you want something?" Ask open-ended questions to help encourage empathy. Let's say your child's friend Jamal can't find his favorite toy car. You can ask your child, "How can we help Jamal feel better about his toy car?" Your child may think of a meaningful way to show kindness—give him a hug, or find another toy.

Above all, be a kind and empathic role model. Demonstrate nonverbal and verbal strategies, and initiate caring gestures such as a hug, a kiss, or holding a hand. Use a soft, calming voice as you let a child know you understand how they feel.

Learning to apologize—which we'll discuss in the pages ahead—is an important part of developing empathy. Regrettably, many parents attempt to teach their kids how to apologize by rote— that is, they provide no context or insight into what it means to apologize. Instead, they let the child figure it out for themselves. For example, if little Billy pushes Suzy into the mud, making her cry, Billy's parent may rush over and say, "Billy, that was a terrible thing you did! Tell Suzy you're sorry. Say, 'I'm sorry, Suzy.'"

Billy, having no choice, stammers, "I'm sorry, Suzy."

While he may have learned the mechanics of making an apology, he hasn't learned the *meaning*. It's been a transaction: a push in the mud in exchange for an embarrassing command from mom to mouth certain words.

Five and Six

At this age, children have more self-awareness and are able to verbalize their feelings about themselves and others. As they become more aware of their own emotions, they in turn, begin to recognize them in others, and their emotional vocabulary expands. Their increased verbal skills allow discussions about emotions that can come from personal experience, a shared reading of a book, a current event, a classroom situation, a picture, or a movie that elicits an emotional response.

Children want to talk about how they feel. They're also improving their skills at reading the feelings of others through their facial expressions, gestures, and actions, as well as understanding the words they say. Parents can encourage the development of empathy by asking children to help each other or a parent with a simple task, to care for a pet, or to do something nice for someone who is ill or has suffered a setback, especially during a holiday when the child may have no clue that many other people cannot share in the happy mood.

Empathy, a Non-Cognitive Prosocial Skill, Should Be Learned Early

While human beings can learn and evolve over the course of an entire lifetime, it's commonly believed that various psychological traits, among them being empathy, need to be rooted in early childhood. This premise was borne out by Drs. Damon E. Jones, Mark Greenberg, and Max Crowley in their report entitled "Early Social-Emotional Functioning and Public Health: The Relationship Between Kindergarten Social Competence and Future Wellness." They sought to determine whether the ratings by kindergarten teachers of their young students' prosocial skills (behaviors intended to help other people, and exhibiting a concern for the rights, feelings, and welfare of others) were predictive of key adolescent and adult outcomes. Their goal was to determine a direct link over and above another important child, family, and contextual characteristics.

The school setting provided the opportunity to observe children's abilities to interact interpersonally as they cooperated with others to complete daily tasks and resolve conflicts. The data came from a long-term study called the Fast Track Project, and the researchers were able to use assessments first made in kindergarten and then thirteen to nineteen years later. They found "statistically significant associations between measured social-emotional skills in kindergarten and key young adult outcomes across multiple domains of education, employment, criminal activity, substance use, and mental health." The study focused on non-cognitive skills, which include memory, attention, planning, language, emotional maturity, empathy, interpersonal skills, and verbal and non-verbal communication. It confirmed previous research that had shown the future likelihood of a person committing a crime was greatly influenced by non-cognitive processes in development including externalizing behavior, social empathy, and effectively regulating emotions. In addition, non-cognitive ability in the form of self-control in childhood was predictive of adult outcomes including physical health, crime, and substance abuse. The researchers concluded, "Our study demonstrates the unique predictive nature of early social competence on important outcomes in late adolescence and early adulthood."

If you want your child to become an adult who is happy, loving, self-sufficient, and engaged in life, it's never too soon to get them started on the right path.

Chapter 8: Daycare and the Myth of Socialization

Before the Industrial Revolution—that is to say, during tens of thousands of years of human history—the vast majority of people lived and worked on farms. Life on a farm was not like today's life in the suburbs. Living on a farm, your daily job site was outside your front door or a short walk across the fields. Your "commute" took about two minutes. On a farm, there were many tasks that children could—and often were required to—perform. And farm families tended to be multi-generational, with grandparents living under the same roof as their grandchildren.

In terms of the care and supervision of young children, these conditions made daycare a non-issue. Babies were simply carried around or stayed in the house with a caregiver—an older sibling or grandparent. Children who were old enough to perform simple tasks such as weeding, hoeing, or picking were put to work right alongside the adults. There was no question of who took care of the child while the parents were at work because *everyone* worked. When kids were old enough, they might have been sent to school, but that was seasonal and the school was likely nearby.

The effect of this lifestyle was twofold. It formed families with close bonds between members, and it immersed even the youngest children in the grown-up world. Children were given responsibilities according to their ability to shoulder them, which meant that sometimes teenagers were given the opportunity—or forced to—function as adults. For example, George Washington was born in 1732; when his father died in 1743, when George was eleven years old, he inherited the family farm at Ferry Farm, Virginia. Early in 1748, George accompanied his brother's father-in-law, George William Fairfax, and James Genn, surveyor of Prince William County, on a month-long trip west across the Blue Ridge Mountains to survey land for Thomas, Lord Fairfax, 6th Baron Cameron. The next year, at the age of seventeen, he received his surveyor's license from the College of William & Mary. Fairfax then appointed him surveyor of Culpeper County, Virginia.

What were you doing when you were seventeen years old? No need to answer that…

The Industrial Revolution, which also brought the mechanization of agriculture, changed how most of us worked and where we lived. People started leaving the farm and moving into cities, and then, after the Second World War, into suburbs. In the United States, before the Civil War about 85 percent of the population was rural and only 15 percent urban. By 1920, less than half of the population lived in rural areas, and by 1930 the proportion had further decreased until it was slightly less than 44 percent. In 1940, less than one in four of the total population lived on farms.

Today, roughly two percent of Americans live on a farm. Of the other 98 percent, 62.7 percent live in cities, and the rest live in "non-metro" areas including small towns and suburbs. The vast majority of people work outside of the home; and according to the Brookings Institute, over 81 percent of Americans drive to work every day.

In addition, we're seeing a rise in single-parent homes. According to Pew Research, the share of US children living with an unmarried parent has more than doubled since 1968, jumping from 13 percent to 32 percent in 2017. That trend has been accompanied by a drop in the share of children living with two married parents, down from 85 percent in 1968 to 65 percent.

What this means is that today, it's nearly certain if you have a child (or two or three), and you work outside the home, you cannot bring your child with you to your place of employment. Companies have been slow to offer daycare for the children of employees; according to *The Outline,* while exact numbers are hard to find, experts estimate no more than eight percent of employers offer on-site childcare as a benefit. Out of the Fortune 100 companies, which are ranked by revenue, just seventeen offer some form of on-site daycare.

The US National Institute of Child Health and Human Development (NICHD) *Study of Early Child Care and Youth Development - Findings for Children up to Age 4 1/2 Years,* published in 2006, found that in the early 1990s, the majority of children began some non-maternal care by six months of age. Results from the study, which included over 1,000 children, showed that the average child spent 27 hours a week in non-maternal care over the first 4½ years of life. During the children's first two years of life, most childcare took place in family homes with relatives or in childcare homes; as children got older, more were in center-based care.

The Great Daycare Debate

The bottom line is this: It's very likely that while you're at work, you're going to need to find someone to care for your child. If, like many parents, in seeking answers you Google "when should a baby start daycare," you're going to see pages of responses that may confuse you even more.

I Googled it, and among many responses, I found this viewpoint on Parents.com:

"The optimal age to begin daycare is just after the child's first birthday… by the age of twelve months, most children have passed through their first wave of separation anxiety, which usually peaks at about nine months."

On the Texas Children's Academy website:

"Research has shown that the best age for a child to start a daycare at is at least twelve months old. Now, just because that is the earliest age many people say is acceptable, that does not mean that your child will be ready for daycare that early. The biggest consideration you need to keep in mind is how your child reacts to being away from you."

Dona Matthews, PhD, writing in *Psychology Today*:

"A quick recap of the research to date: For the first three years, infants and toddlers do best in home-based settings. They tend to experience less stress, less illness, and fewer behavioral problems."

The NIHD study said:

"Children with higher quantity (total combined number of hours) of experience in non-maternal child care showed somewhat more behavior problems in child care and in kindergarten classrooms than those who had experienced fewer hours."

On WorkingMother.com, writer Audrey Goodson Kingo produced a slew of research studies claiming that high-quality daycare is *superior* to home care:

• Behavior: Kids who attend "high-quality, center-based childcare" exhibit "better behaviors" than those who don't.

• Cancer: Kids who had been in daycare were less likely to have acute leukemia than those who had only been at home.

• College: Infants enrolled in a high-quality childcare program were four times more likely to have earned a college degree.

• Career: By the age of thirty, kids who had been in high-quality care were more likely to have been consistently employed.

Obviously, the mission of any publication calling itself Working Mother will be to make working mothers feel good about leaving their children in daycare. You can't expect them to present any research that would make the working mother feel guilty.

There's also a high dose of subjectivity to this question. Everyone agrees that the *quality* of time is just as important as the *quantity* of time with your child. That is to say, if a child is being raised in a crack house and the parent or caregiver lives a chaotic, dangerous life, that child would be better off spending as much time as possible in high-quality daycare. The comparisons between daycare and home life should only be made on a level playing field—good daycare versus a good home life.

Socialization

One of the most common arguments offered in support of daycare is that the child needs the benefit of socialization.

Merriam Webster's Medical Dictionary provides the following definition of socialization:

"The process by which a human being beginning at infancy acquires the habits, beliefs, and accumulated knowledge of society through education and training for adult status."

You want your child to become an adult who is happy, loving, self-sufficient, and engaged in life. This means raising an emotionally well-adjusted child who can interact socially and function in group settings. What parent wants to knowingly raise a socially backward child who is uncomfortable interacting with others? To allay these fears, parents may turn to daycare and preschool, where the educational opportunities presumably allow "normal" socialization to develop.

As a working parent, you may not have the luxury of many choices. You need to work to pay the rent and put food on the table. Staying home with your child may not be an option.

Notwithstanding that reality, I believe that if at all possible, parents should find a way to keep their child at home, and not in daycare. This is because in the early years before pre-school or kindergarten, nothing is more important than building a strong bond between mother and child or father and child. Many parents will justify sending their kids to daycare by saying to themselves and to others that daycare will be good because their children will acquire socialization skills. The truth is that four- and five-year-old kids will have the rest of their lives to develop socialization skills. It's much more important for infants and toddlers to develop a strong, loving emotional bond with at least one primary parent caretaker.

Many parents keep their children out of daycare—and indeed, out of the established school system—because for them, "socialization" is another word for "conformity." They see the goal of the school system to be the production of dutiful workers who are trained to show up, shut up, and do their job. They point to quotes such as this one, from William Torrey Harris, US Commissioner of Education from 1889 to 1906, in which he expressed the vision of socialization in his 1889 book *Philosophy of Education*:

"Ninety-nine [students] out of a hundred are automata, careful to walk in prescribed paths, careful to follow the prescribed custom. This is not an accident but the result of substantial education, which, scientifically defined, is the subsumption of the individual."

They argue that our system of education is an artificial contrivance, and in particular point to the arbitrary grouping of children into age-determined peer groups. Where else in life, they say, are people segregated by age? As Brent and Stacey-jean Inion wrote in "Socialization: Debunking the Myth," our system of education stifles inter-generational interaction. "Where are the grandmothers," they ask, "who are content to pass down heirloom recipes and traditions? Where are the young men who look to grandfathers to teach them a trade? Industrialization has wiped out the vital role senior adults once had in the US culture." They have a point; in the real working world, new hires fresh out of college rub elbows with more experienced workers. On the farm, all generations work together. In families, parents and children sit at the same table. Only in the classroom do we group children by age, and this is purely for expediency and lower cost. It's cheaper to teach twenty kids the same lesson than try to do it individually, or in mixed groups.

The Strong Parental Bond

Whether you choose to place your child in daycare or keep them at home, the one thing to remember is that there is no replacement for a strong bond between you and your child.

As Robert Winston and Rebecca Chicot wrote in "The importance of early bonding on the long-term mental health and resilience of children," from the moment of birth, human babies are very dependent on their parents. During the first two years of life, they experience massive brain development, growth, and neuron pruning. Just like a garden needs tending for optimal growth, so does the child's brain, as well as their social, emotional and cognitive development. A loving bond or attachment relationship with a primary caregiver, usually a parent, makes a significant difference. They wrote that evidence is mounting from the fields of developmental psychology, neurobiology, and animal epigenetic studies that "neglect, parental inconsistency, and a lack of love can lead to long-term mental health problems as well as to reduced overall potential and happiness."

We're talking not just about a feeling or supposition that parental love and attention are important, but about significant changes in brain chemistry and neural wiring that occur when infants and children are consistently stimulated by a loving and affirmative caregiver. Winston and Chicot noted a study by M. Rutter and others of children from a Romanian orphanage that took in infants, cared for them as they grew, and then successfully placed them in loving homes. When each child was six years old, the researchers assessed what proportion of these adopted children were functioning "normally." They found that:

• 69 percent of the children adopted before they reached the age of six months were functioning normally

• 43 percent of the children adopted between the ages of seven months and two years were functioning normally

• 22 percent of the children adopted between the ages of two years and 3.5 years were functioning normally

That is to say, the longer a child stayed in the orphanage—which, no matter how professionally operated, was no substitute for a loving family—the further behind they fell developmentally.

And it's not about the material things that you buy. They wrote, "Parents can worry about things that just aren't important to their children's brain development and well-being, such as giving them their own room, buying them toys, and taking them on expensive holidays. Instead, the most valuable gift that a child can receive is free; it's simply a parent's love, time and support. This is no empty sentiment; science is now showing why baby's brains need love more than anything else."

John Bowlby's Attachment Theory

John Bowlby was a twentieth-century psychoanalyst who believed that many mental health and behavioral problems could be attributed to adverse conditions in early childhood. His evolutionary theory of attachment suggests that infants come into the world biologically pre-programmed to form attachments with others because this will help them survive. These attachment behaviors are instinctive and are activated by any conditions that seem to threaten the attachment, such as separation, insecurity, and fear.

His theory has five main points.

1. An infant forms one primary attachment, and this "attachment figure"—usually the mother—acts as a secure base for exploring the world. Moreover, the relationship with the attachment figure acts as a prototype for all future social relationships, so disrupting it can have severe consequences.

(You've probably heard this admonition about young men: "If you want to know how a man will treat his wife, look at how he treats his mother." There's no better proof of the attachment theory.)

2. This "monotropy" needs to last for at least the first two years of the child's life.

3. Short-term separation from the attachment figure leads to distress in three progressive stages:

Protest: The child cries, screams and protests angrily when the parent leaves. They will try to cling on to the parent to stop them from leaving.

Despair: The child's protesting begins to stop, and they appear to be calmer although still upset. The child refuses others' attempts for comfort and often seems withdrawn and uninterested in anything.

Detachment: If the separation continues the child will start to engage with other people again. They will reject the caregiver on their return and show strong signs of anger.

4. The long-term consequences of deprivation from the attachment figure might include the following:
- delinquency
- reduced intelligence
- increased aggression
- depression
- affectionless psychopathy—the inability to care about or feel affection for others

5. The child's attachment relationship with their primary caregiver leads to the development of an internal working model. A child's future interaction with others is guided by memories and expectations from this internal model, which influences and helps evaluate their contacts with others.

The 44 Thieves Study

Between 1936 and 1939, a group of 88 children were selected from the clinic where Bowlby worked. Of these, 44 were juvenile thieves and had been referred to him because of their stealing. Bowlby selected another group of 44 children to act as controls. They had been referred to the clinic for various reasons, but none had committed any crimes.

After a series of psychological tests, checks of police records, and interviews with the children and their parents, Bowlby found that during their first five years of life, more than half of the juvenile thieves had been separated from their mothers for longer than six months. In the control group, only two had had such a separation.

He also found fourteen of the young thieves showed affectionless psychopathy. None of the control group showed this disorder. Of the fourteen affectionless psychopaths, twelve had spent most of their early years in residential homes or hospitals and were not often visited by their families.

Bowlby concluded that separation or deprivation from the attachment figure in the child's early life caused permanent emotional damage.

Do the Best You Can

I don't want to put working parents on a guilt trip. Life is tough enough without some shrink giving you a lecture about how you should quit your job and stay home with your child because if you don't, he'll grow up to be Charles Manson. After all, the title of this book is *Affirmative Parenting*, not *Impossible Parenting*.

Despite the vast differences in parental advice served up by the internet, every expert agrees that the quality of the time you spend with your child is very important. If it's a few hours a day before and after work, you owe it to yourself and your child to make them count.

And—miracle of miracles—experts also agree that the quality of your family time has nothing to do with contrived or costly vacations or activities. In other words, just going for a walk in the park with your child is valuable and will enhance your attachment. As researchers, Tamar Kremer-Sadlik and Amy L. Paugh wrote in "Everyday Moments: Finding 'quality time' in American working families," our current American cultural climate insists that "quality time" is important for family well-being. However, such pressure often engenders stress and guilt among working parents, who have difficulty finding time for "quality time." After interviewing 32 two-parent working families, they found that "everyday activities (like household chores or running errands) may afford families quality moments—those unplanned, unstructured instances of social interaction that serve the important relationship-building functions parents seek from 'quality time.'"

Citing previous research, the study's authors argued that children often value those regular moments more than the elaborate, scheduled, "fun" occasions. If you, the harried parent, need to go to the supermarket—take your child. If you need to wash the dishes, ask your child to help, or just chat while you work. Raking leaves? Involve the little one.

At the risk of sounding bossy, I must insist on one thing: When you are with your child, whether they are two years old or twenty, you *must turn off your electronics*.

• No phones

- No internet
- No video games

Everyone likes movies, but going to a movie with your child or watching television with them is *not quality time*. Sorry, it just isn't. Staring at a screen with someone does not bring you closer. If you want a shared spectator activity, then take your child to a sporting event, where you can sit together and talk about the game and how the referee must have been blind not to see that flagrant foul perpetrated against the guy on our team.

When you're with your child, keep your phone in your pocket or purse. At the dinner table, prohibit the use of phones.

Aside from shared activities and chores inside the house, the next best thing is to get out of the house and into nature. In their paper "The Effects of the Natural Environment on Attention and Family Cohesion: An Experimental Study," researchers Dina Izenstark and Aaron T. Ebata studied the benefits of spending time in nature as a family and found that exposure to nature, when experienced by a family, has a powerful effect on relationships. The benefits relate to your ability to *pay attention*.

First developed by Rachel and Stephen Kaplan, Attention Restoration Theory (ART) describes how interaction with natural environments can reduce mental fatigue and restore attentional functioning. "When your attention is restored, you're able to pick up on social cues more easily, you feel less irritable, and you have more self-control. All of these are variables that can help you get along better with others," said Dina Izenstark, lead author of the study.

Kaplan and Kaplan propose that the natural environment is a particularly valuable context because it often has the four characteristics that encourage restored attention:

1) Extent: the scope to feel immersed in the environment

2) Being away: providing an escape from habitual activities

3) Soft fascination: aspects of the environment that capture attention effortlessly

4) Compatibility: Individuals must want to be exposed to, and appreciate the environment

This doesn't have to be a big, expensive vacation to the mountains—it can be as ordinary as walking the dog together every evening. It's a simple activity, but one that brings a sense of belonging and identity to family members.

Chapter 9: Potty Training

The goals of potty or toilet training are deceptively simple:

1. Teach the child to recognize when he or she needs to defecate or urinate.

2. Instead of simply "lettin' it rip" into the handy and heretofore always-ready diaper, the child must hold the urge, hurry to a parent-approved potty, sit down (or stand up), and unload into the basin.

3. When the child is finished, clean oneself with the parent-approved toilet paper.

4. And then wash their hands.

When you think about it, in terms of human development, toilet training is a huge step forward. It represents a significant leap in learning how to be aware of the processes within one's own body, and then to exert control over them. Other wild mammals that need to acquire specialized skills such as hunting or burrow-building don't need to learn about potty training; they just go whenever and wherever the urge strikes. As far as we know, humans are the only species that demands its children learn to excrete only in certain approved places, and if necessary, to "hold it in" until such a place is accessible.

Most parents, eager to rid themselves of the effort and expense of changing diapers, are greatly relieved when their child has reached and mastered this important life milestone. When the child first does it successfully, the adults grab their phones and excitedly call the older relatives: "Guess what? Junior did it *in the potty*! What a happy day!"

But no loving parent wants their child to be traumatized by the training experience. It seems like a tricky business—you want to get it done, but you have to be careful about it.

It's no wonder, then, that if you Google "potty training," you'll see a dizzying array of advice columns and helpful tips that all seem to say something different.

Here are the basics.

The number one rule is this: Relax.

Ask yourself: Have you ever seen a grown adult human being who was *not* toilet trained?

If your social circles are anything like mine, I'm sure you'll answer in the negative. All of your adult friends and business associates are toilet trained, even if they often seem to lack other basic life skills. Therefore, one may conclude that toilet training is something that every human—all seven billion of us—eventually learns and masters.

Your child will be no exception. Your child will "get it," just like every other child from here to Tibet, and all points in between. The only variable is the age at which they learn.

When Do We Start?

This is probably the number one question every parent asks.

While many children show signs of being ready for potty training between ages eighteen months and two years, others—even those who seem to be otherwise developmentally advanced for their age—might not be ready until they're three years old.

The answer to the question is, "Your child will let you know."

Not literally, of course, although it's conceivable that throughout history, some children have marched up to a parent and announced, "Mommy, I'm ready to be toilet trained." Anything's possible, but it's still unlikely.

Here are six questions you can ask yourself to help determine if your child is ready:

1. Can my child understand and follow basic directions?
2. Can my child identify and sit on a kiddie toilet?
3. Can my child pull down his or her pants and pull them up again?
4. Can my child refrain from peeing for up to two hours?
5. Does my child seem interested in using the toilet or wearing "big-kid" underwear?
6. Can my child communicate when he or she needs to go?

If you answered mostly "yes," your child might be ready. If you answered mostly "no," then you might want to wait.

You can also look for these signs:

1. You're changing fewer wet diapers. Until the age of about twenty months, kids pee frequently and without any outward signs. But if you notice that when you check the diaper, it's been dry for a few hours; this is a sign the toddler may be physically ready for potty training.

2. Your child's poops are predictable. Young toddlers seem to have unpredictable bowel movements, but as the months go by, they may become more regular, giving you the ability to pace your child's visits to the bathroom.

3. He or she announces their bodily functions. Some kids proudly announce when poop is coming. But the message isn't always verbal; every parent of a toilet-trained child remembers the "pee-pee dance," usually accompanied by an expression of desperate anguish on the child's face. Regardless of the form of communication, if your child shows she's aware of her bodily functions, she's ready for potty training.

4. They understand bathroom vocabulary. Your child is ready for potty training if they understand and are able to use the family's words for bathroom functions and any associated body parts.

5. He dislikes a dirty diaper. Most toddlers go through a phase where they become keenly aware of cleanliness. They'll help you wipe the tray on their high chair, or complain of sticky hands. This is a good opportunity to initiate the potty-training discussion because he'll be receptive to the idea of not wearing stinky diapers.

6. She can undress quickly. While the parent or caregiver will likely be present for the first few months of training, a key to eventual self-sufficiency is for the child to be able to pull down his or her pants and then pull them back up.

7. They can wash their own hands. Part of the training process is to help the child wash his or her own hands after using the potty. This habit needs to be ingrained from an early age and carried through life.

The process of potty training is simple, as long as you keep a cheerful and pragmatic demeanor. Get a kiddie potty and put it in the bathroom. Tell your toddler what it's for. Let them sit on it. When you change the diaper, take the opportunity to invite your child to sit on the potty and "practice." Eventually, your child will try it herself, or tell you she wants to try it. During the training period—anywhere from a few weeks to a year—you can expect false starts and a few accidents.

As an affirmative parent, your job is to keep a smile on your face. When your child successfully uses the potty, give him or her a big hug and say, "Good for you!" If your child has an accident, clean it up and say, "That's okay, we'll just try again!"

Avoid dramatics. Convey to your child that poop and pee are perfectly normal, but that we need to keep them separate from ourselves. Please don't force your child to sit on the potty until "something comes out." That would be absurd for an adult, and just as absurd for a child.

It is 100% guaranteed that your child will eventually become proficient at using the potty, just like her parents. The only questions are how long it will take and whether the process will be pleasant or traumatic. The answer to the first question is that no one knows how long it will take; the answer to the second question is entirely up to you.

Chapter 10: Temper Tantrums

Everyone has witnessed this scene:

You're in a department store or supermarket. It's crowded with shoppers. Suddenly you hear the unmistakable sound of a child's desperate wailing. It cuts through the air like a knife. You think, what's going on? Is a child being kidnapped? You discreetly look around the corner. There, in the aisle, you see an adult—let's say it's a woman, presumably the child's mother, but it could just as well be the dad—bending down to speak to a child who is writhing on the floor. The mother is trying not to draw attention to herself and this embarrassing family drama, while the child has exactly the opposite goal—to be the center of the world's attention. You catch snippets of an exchange:

Parent: "No, you cannot have that toy."

Child: "But I WAAANNT it!"

Parent: "Not today. I need you to get up off the floor. Stop all that screaming."

Child: "But I WAAANNT it!"

And so on. Sometimes you think, "Oh that poor parent, I feel so sorry for her." Other times you think, "Boy, that parent is being a real jerk," especially if the parent becomes angry and physically drags the child out the door.

What would you do if *your* child threw a tantrum in a public place?

I hope that as an affirmative parent, you would respond with grace and patience, and not be swayed by what you're imagining the onlookers are thinking. If they aren't parents or caregivers themselves, they will never understand; and if they are parents, they ought to have some empathy.

In any case, I also hope that from infancy, you've been building with your child the kind of trusting and loving relationship that will make childhood tantrums infrequent and mild. A tantrum is a sign of panic. When children become emotionally charged—for whatever reason—they can't think straight. They cannot function normally. They want seemingly trivial things and are unsatisfied with any attempt to give them an alternative.

At such times, your child needs your steady patience. They can't get out of that state without your help.

And—this may be hard to accept, but it's true—sometimes the best thing you can do for a child gripped by a tantrum is to step away from your child and wait.

While the loving and well-meaning parent may respond to an outburst by offering soothing words of comfort, this response is often met with *increased* yelling, anger, and acting out.

Why?

When a child throws a tantrum, they want your attention. They want to control your actions and be the center of your world. If tantrums are like fires, then providing attention is the fuel that keeps them burning. (Remember, we're talking about a tantrum, not about a traumatic experience, which requires your quick response and soothing touch. When your child falls, cuts her knee, and begins to wail, this is your cue to swoop in and offer comfort.)

The best response is to stay near your child to ensure they don't do anything destructive, like pull stuff off the shelves of the store. If possible, usher them to a quiet spot. The movement may trigger an increased outburst, so it's your call as to whether it's a worthwhile strategy. Once you're where you want to be, remain calm and detached. Say nothing. Don't feed the fire. If onlookers catch your eye, say, "He's okay—just blowing off steam," or, "Sorry to bother you, but she'll cool off soon."

Eventually, the fire will burn out and your child will calm down. Reward your child for this shift. Bend down and say, "Ah, I see you're ready to come back to mommy. Yes?"

If the child responds with more thrashing, look away and say, "I'll wait." Then say no more.

The message to your child should be: "I'm your loving parent and I will never *abandon* you, but on the other hand I'm not going to reward you for your behavior." Your child needs to learn that he or she will never benefit from throwing a tantrum, and that good behavior brings bountiful love and affection.

Looking at the big picture, you can do a lot to prevent tantrums in the first place. A child throws a tantrum because he or she feels desperate. He or she *must* have that toy or *must* be allowed to watch that TV show, otherwise they will *die*. The question is, why should so much importance be placed on one thing? A child who has *choices* won't be so threatened if one choice is denied. Instead of just saying "no" to what the child wants, offer an acceptable alternative.

If the child refuses to leave the playground, say, "Don't worry—we'll come back to the playground tomorrow. The swings will still be here."

If the child demands a toy, say, "That looks like a very good idea for a birthday present!" Or, "We're not buying that toy today, but when we get home I'll play robot with you. How does that sound?"

In general, if you allow your child to make her own innocuous choices throughout the day, if a moment comes when she has no choice, then it won't seem so threatening. The stakes won't seem so high because denying her this one choice—to buy the toy in the store—won't seem like a threat to her identity, and she'll shrug and move on to something else.

Look at it this way. If you were hungry and went to a restaurant, and the server said, "I'm sorry, we're out of chicken, but we have plenty of steak and fish and everything else," it probably wouldn't bother you because you had other choices. But if the server said, "I'm sorry, we're out of chicken, and we have *nothing else*," you'd probably throw a tantrum too.

Behavioral Disorders

If despite your best efforts, tantrums are persistent and exhausting for you, it's possible your child may have a behavioral disorder.

• **Anxiety disorders** can manifest in various ways, including generalized anxiety disorder (excessive worrying), panic disorder (anxiety attacks), and separation anxiety disorder (excessive anxiety away from home or when separated from parents or caregivers).

• **Attention-deficit/hyperactivity disorder (ADHD)** is marked by an ongoing pattern of inattention and/or hyperactivity-impulsivity that interferes with functioning or development.

• **Disruptive mood dysregulation disorder (DMDD)** may be a cause of chronic anger. Parents walk around on tiptoes, hoping not to set off a temper tantrum. Between temper tantrums, the child may be irritable and angry throughout the day.

• **Oppositional defiant disorder (ODD)** is characterized by a pattern of negative, hostile or defiant behavior that might include temper tantrums, arguing, being easily annoyed, and other disruptive behaviors over a period of six months or more.

• **Sensory processing problems** may lead to emotional outbursts—what mental health professionals refer to as "emotional dysregulation"—when the child feels overwhelmed.

• **Learning disabilities** may lead a child to act out to divert attention away from their struggle.

The occasional tantrum is to be expected from a healthy child testing the limits of parental patience. If despite your sincere attempts to build your child's self-confidence your child has difficulty maintaining self-control or simply enjoying life, then consult your pediatrician.

Please be very careful about diagnosis and treatment. Before resorting to medications, explore every possible non-medication therapy.

This has become a particularly acute issue when children are diagnosed with ADHD.

It seems as though ADHD has become rampant in our society. According to the ADD Resource Center, during their lifetimes, 12.9 percent of men will be diagnosed with attention disorder, as well as 4.9 percent of women. The CDC says that 11 percent of American children ages four to seventeen—6.4 million—have the attention disorder. That's an increase of 42 percent in just eight years.

The exact causes of ADHD are not yet clear, and research efforts continue. Factors that may be involved in the development of ADHD include genetics, the environment, or problems with the central nervous system at key moments in development.

As of this writing, 6.1 percent of all American children are being treated for ADHD with medication. The National Center for Health Statistics reported that 7.5 percent of U.S. children between ages six and seventeen were taking medication for overall "emotional or behavioral difficulties" in 2011-2012.

That's a lot of drugs and a lot of money, too. A study from 2007 reported that the "cost of illness" for a person with ADHD is $14,576 each year. That means ADHD costs Americans 42.5 billion dollars each year—and that's on the conservative side of ADHD prevalence estimates. Globally, Grand View Research has reported the global market for ADHD medications is expected to reach $24.9 billion by 2025.

I'm not anti-medication. I believe that with issues of children's behavior, every other option should be explored and tried before turning to medications. We're talking about behavior, which unlike an infectious disease or cancer carries no identifying biomarker. There is no blood test or CAT scan that can diagnose ADHD. What one parent might consider dangerous hyperactivity, another might consider healthy exuberance. In a field without biomarkers, there is a risk of subjective diagnosis, inviting unnecessary treatment and over-medication.

The Centers for Disease Control and Prevention (CDC) endorses the position of the American Academy of Pediatrics (AAP), which states that for children diagnosed with ADHD younger than six years of age, the first line of treatment should be parent training in behavior management before medication is tried. For children six years of age and older, the recommendations include medication and behavior therapy together—parent training in behavior management for children up to age twelve, and other types of behavior therapy and training for adolescents.

Schools can be part of the treatment plan as well. AAP recommendations include adding behavioral classroom intervention and school supports.

Chapter 11: Morality and Conscience

The upright character and high moral virtues of our first president, George Washington, have been transformed into myth by the tale of the cherry tree.

According to the story, when George was but six-years-old he received a hatchet as a gift. He promptly went outside and hacked at his father's cherry tree. When his father discovered what George had done, he became angry and confronted him. Young George bravely said, "I cannot tell a lie: I did cut it with my hatchet." George's father embraced him and rejoiced that his son's honesty was worth more than a thousand trees.

The incident is both touching and inspiring, but it never happened. The story was invented by one of George Washington's first biographers, Mason Locke Weems, in the 1806 edition of *The Life of Washington*.

Recently, a first-grader of our acquaintance, upon learning the tale was fiction, exclaimed, "I knew it! How ironic that a story extolling the virtues of honesty should itself be a cynical lie!"

(Actually, no first-grader said that. I made it up. I thought it sounded good.)

We live in a world of mixed messages about truth-telling. On one hand, we insist that our children tell the truth at every occasion, even if it's painful, while on the other hand, they see big, important adults on television blithely telling lies about even the most ordinary things. They also see their parents indulge in useful fibs. How often do we say when the phone rings, "If that's Uncle George, please tell him I'm not home," or, "Don't tell mommy you saw me eating this chocolate cake, okay?"

Regardless of the current zeitgeist regarding truth-telling, as well as the willingness of adults to promote "harmless" lies, the fact is that children often cannot see any moral difference between what they know is true and what they know isn't true. This is not a moral defect; it's just the way their brains are wired (or not wired, as the case may be).

Children of all ages lie with an amazing facility. Their propensity for lying often seems to get worse as they enter adolescence and their lies become increasingly bold and consequential.

Let's take a closer look at why kids lie and how you can steer them towards a path of honesty.

The Lying Time Line

As a parent, you can expect a child to evolve in their ability to lie, their willingness to do so, and their skill at succeeding in it.

Infants generally lack the verbal skills to lie, and if you're a parent you know that whatever comes out of the mouth of your two-year-old is likely to be a mishmash of recognizable words and nonsensical babbling. Children who are just learning to speak get a pass on lying because half the time you can't even tell what they're saying.

By the time children are three years old, they're better at articulating their thoughts—and they start telling little lies. This may surprise you, but from a developmental perspective, lying is often one of the first signs a young child has developed a "theory of mind," which is the awareness others may have different desires, feelings, and beliefs to oneself. When a child misleadingly claims, "Daddy said I could have a cookie," they're using this new-found awareness of others' minds to plant false knowledge. While lying itself may be socially unacceptable, the understanding that others are thinking and feeling in their minds and hearts is an important social skill. It's related to empathy, the ability to cooperate, and caring for others when they're in distress.

To make matters even more complicated, we encourage our children to use their imaginations and engage in play-acting. Here's an example. Your two-year-old comes into the room, crawling on her hands and knees and meowing. Amused, you look down and say, "Are you a cat?"

The child replies, "Yes, I'm a cat."

Or your child climbs into a cardboard box and you ask, "What is that you're in?"

Your child answers, "A boat! I'm going fishing."

Is that lying? Of course not. But it certainly isn't literal truth-telling. It's healthy evidence that your child has developed a sense of identity and can imagine herself being a cat, or that a cardboard box is a boat. We, adults, applaud such imaginative thinking and praise our children for doing it. We should be able to forgive young children if they apply those same skills to telling a fib about getting a cookie, and gently instruct them in the difference between imaginative play-acting and making false statements when we ask for the facts.

Children also begin to learn that adults don't know everything. This is an important discovery. In realizing they have their own identity, separate from the big hairy caregivers, children also realize adults sometimes ask questions for which they don't know the answer. For example, mommy will ask Suzy, "Did you brush your teeth?" thus indicating to Suzy that mommy doesn't know the answer. If Suzy doesn't want to brush her teeth, she hopes that the answer of "yes" might be accepted and get her off the hook.

Strong emotions, combined with a strong sense of self-interest, can make a child insist, "I never got my cookie!" when you know they did. Remember that toddlers are trying to exhibit their independence and they can make a power struggle out of any disagreement. They're too young to be punished for lying, but parents can subtly begin to encourage truthfulness by gently getting the child to agree to what the parent knows is the truth. So you can say, "You didn't get a cookie? But I gave one to you. I saw you eat it. Isn't that right?" Most little kids will quickly back down and switch to another tactic, such as, "Yes, but I should get *another* one."

Young children are more apt to tell the truth about something they did that they weren't supposed to do. In their study, "Development of lying to conceal a transgression: Children's control of expressive behavior during verbal deception," Victoria Talwar and Kang Lee assembled a group of children ages three to seven. In a "temptation resistance paradigm," each child was left alone in a room with a music-playing Barney toy placed behind their back. The children were told not to peek at the toy. Of course, most of the kids could not resist temptation and peeked. When the experimenter asked them whether they had peeked, about half of the three-year-olds confessed they had done so, whereas most older children lied and denied peeking. The willingness to lie increased with age, possibly because the older kids were more aware of the fact that they had done something wrong that could bring punishment and therefore sought to evade the long arm of the law.

The researchers noted, "Whereas the majority of the children between three and five years blurted out the name of the toy that they denied having peeked at, and thus implicated themselves as having transgressed, about half of the six- and seven-year-olds feigned ignorance of the toy's identity."

Interestingly, a group of "naïve" adults who were not familiar with the experiment were shown videotapes of the children. Based on the kids' nonverbal expressive behaviors, the adults could not differentiate the liars from the truth-tellers. However, the children were poor at "semantic leakage control" and the adults could correctly identify most of the lie-tellers based on their verbal statements made in the same context as the lie. Many of the younger kids blurted out the name "Barney," which they could not have known unless they had peeked. In contrast, older children who successfully feigned ignorance were not distinguishable from children who did not peek, and they were not detected by adults.

Researchers distinguish between "first-order" lying and "second-order" lying. The former involves a simple denial of a fact: "I did not look at the toy." But a second-order lie requires the child to construct a lie in layers. For example, as the researchers wrote, "to sustain the lie that one had not peeked, when asked the identity of the object they were told not to peek at, children had to infer what belief they ought to have, given the initial denial." In other words, when asked follow-up questions, the child who simply says "I didn't peek at the toy" must then be able to think, "Because I've said I didn't peek, I would therefore not know the name of the toy."

From ages four to six, kids get more skilled at lying by learning to sync their tone of voice and facial expressions to their words. During this period, if instead of getting angry you respectfully ask them to fess up, they'll usually acknowledge the lie. Use the opportunity to explain what a lie is and why it's bad. Be firm and serious, and say, "Are you absolutely sure that's what happened?" or "It sounds like you're not telling the truth." After listening to and gently correcting your child, move on gracefully.

Avoid berating the child unless the situation is serious and requires more attention.

From six to eight, kids will lie more frequently, and are better at it. The lies get more complicated as their language mastery develops, and they understand more about how others think. The introduction of school, and things like homework and classroom discipline, provide fertile ground for the sprouting of tall tales. Children will invent stories to test what they can get away with, especially related to classes, homework, teachers, and friends. At this age, the new reality of rules and responsibilities is often stressful for children. They will often lie to deflect the forces that seem to demand more performance than they can deliver. Fortunately, most lies ("No, mommy, we don't have to read any books this summer") are relatively easy to detect.

By age eight, most children can lie successfully and plausibly. Remember, one reason children lie is that they are engaging in imaginative play. One of the important tasks of childhood is to push boundaries, test the waters, and see what can and can't be done. Often the child will seek to escape the disapproval of the parent by offering a sanitized version of reality: "No, I did not draw on the wall," or "Yes, I ate all of my kale. I did not throw it out the window onto the sidewalk. That pile of kale must have been put there by someone else." Although this can be very frustrating, testing household authority figures helps the child learn about the world and themselves, and—if the tall tales are called out and exposed—develop important social skills.

Parents often wonder if their child knows the difference between telling the truth and lying. It's important for parents to understand this simple but wrenching contradiction: Research has shown that children know the difference between the truth and lying, and they know that lying is wrong—but when given the opportunity, they will happily lie. As Victoria Talwar and colleagues wrote in 2002, "Most children demonstrated appropriate conceptual knowledge of lying and truth-telling and the obligation, to tell the truth, but many of the same children lied to conceal their transgression."

There is good news for parents, though. Talwar and her colleagues noted that without asking children to promise to tell the truth, the majority of children would lie. However, when children were asked to promise to tell the truth, close to 50 percent of the children would tell the truth, making such a procedure ideal for examining the relations between lying and social and cognitive factors. Therefore, when questioning your child—or indeed, anybody—about a transgression, begin by calmly asking them if they intend to tell the truth, and when they say "yes," confirm their agreement, to tell the truth. If you do this, you're more likely to get the truth.

Teenage Lying

By the time the child becomes a teenager, he or she is probably an expert liar. They have confidence in their ability to pull off a lie, enough physical self-control to look you straight in the eye as they do it, and the brainpower to maintain the lie during follow-up questions.

For parents, because the stakes can be high, no teenage behavior is more vexing than lying. The problem is that most teenagers' sense of morality lags far behind their physical and mental capabilities. While parents often view lying as a moral issue, to the adolescent it's merely a practical one, useful for either getting out of trouble or getting to do what is forbidden.

Let's face it—most teenagers are deeply conflicted:

1) They resent the control their parents have over them and believe they're entitled to greater freedoms than mom and dad will grant them. Furthermore, they want to do stuff they know their parents won't like—smoke, have sex, drink alcohol, or just goof off. Life is just so *unfair!*

At the same time...

2) They know, deep down, that despite their bravado, they're not ready to survive in the world on their own. They still need their parents to shelter them, feed them, and help them buy the things they want and need. It's just so *frustrating!*

So, they find a way to keep up appearances with the "parental units" while managing to do the things they want to do. This may require some creative storytelling, which is no problem because no one gets hurt, right?

A big problem, though, can be what many experts call "lifestyle lying." This variety of deception is used to conceal something very private and very damaging. It may include hiding:

- Eating disorders, such as anorexia nervosa and bulimia
- Trichotillomania—the compulsion to pull out one's hair
- Cutting, and other types of self-harm
- A drug dependency
- Flunking out of school, or cutting classes
- Gang affiliation

These are serious issues that may require professional intervention. But the first step in helping a child who is deep into deception is for the *parents to face the facts*. Too many parents, burdened with their problems, are willing to believe their child when the child says, "Don't worry, everything is fine." Many adolescent lifestyle liars are skilled manipulators, easy to believe and easy to forgive. The parents who see a glimpse of reality tell themselves, "She's a good kid. When she gets caught, she's so sweet and repentant. We feel so sorry for her. We think she deserves the benefit of the doubt and another chance." The root of parental denial of adolescent lying is *hope*—hope their suspicions are unfounded, hope that what happened won't happen again, hope that from now on truth will be told, hope their child will magically transform into a responsible adult.

Unfortunately, once a teenager has a serious problem with the truth because of an underlying psychological issue, the solution needs to involve the parents as well. A child who is pulling out her hair and hiding this behavior from her parents needs three things: 1) Parents who are paying closer attention to what their child is doing, and 2) Parents who are willing to invest the time and resources necessary to get their child the treatment they deserve, and 3) Parents who are non-judgmental and are focused only on helping their child to become an adult who is happy, loving, self-sufficient, and engaged in life.

Cults

Teenagers have an intense desire to belong—to a family, a team, a gang, a group of their peers. In most cases, this desire to belong is a healthy one and results in productivity and increased opportunities. Sometimes, as in the case of a gang, it can lead to negative outcomes.

Perhaps nothing is more frightening to a parent than the prospect of their child—usually a teenager or young adult—choosing to join a religious or cultural group that demands complete loyalty, even to the extent of cutting ties with the family.

There are many definitions of the word "cult," so I'll use it in its broadest sense. A cult is an organization that:

- Professes to have exclusive knowledge of some truth about the world, or promotes an exclusive viewpoint that demands the rejection of other viewpoints
- Demands total loyalty from its members, including the severance of ties with "non-believers," including family members
- Seeks to socially and financially isolate the member; for example, by giving the member a new name, claiming the member's assets, and requiring the member to live in a cult-approved compound or residence
- Tests the member's loyalty to the organization and its leader, by assigning various tasks or requiring personally demeaning activities, which may include sexual subjugation

In our society, we tend to view cults as those organizations we *don't* like, whereas the organizations we *do* like are not cults. Some people love the military, while others think the military is like a cult. Many people admire nuns who are members of holy orders, while others take a dimmer view. It's beyond the scope of this book to make those determinations for you. And remember, the ideals of the group are probably quite attractive superficially—such as peace on earth, or promoting the healthy development of brain and body—and offer a contrast to the perceived corruption of the "real" world.

Suffice to say, if your adult child suddenly vanishes and then you learn they've joined a cult, you can take steps to help extricate them.

"Do everything you can to stay in touch," said Janja Lalich, a sociology professor, and consultant who studies cults and coercive influence and control, to reporter Malia Wollan of *The New York Times*. Gently and persistently provide reminders of the outside world by emailing, calling, sending photographs, writing letters, and, if possible, visiting—but only if you're calm enough to not pass judgment and avoid lashing out. Your child chose to join the group, and your child needs to decide to leave. Criticizing the group, however strange or dangerous it seems to you, is the same as criticizing your child. The members love the group, and for all intents and purposes, they *are* the group.

In the late 20th century, families often hired so-called deprogrammers to kidnap and hold cult members against their will. It may have worked, but it's illegal, and a Washington man successfully sued his deprogrammer in 1995. Don't try to forcibly remove your child, even if you're gravely concerned. Today's accepted method is "exit counseling," and it requires persuasion by friends, lawyers, therapists, and family members.

If you can visit your child, ask questions, and be ready to offer evidence that the cult is not a good place to be. "Video testimonials from former cult members can be particularly persuasive," said Lalich,

Above all, keep in mind it's very hard, and often humiliating, for cult members to admit to the outside world that they were wrong. This is why you need to be there as the unconditionally loving and caring parent that you are. Your job is to help your child see that life in the real world is far more interesting and fulfilling than living in a cult, however laudable its goals may appear to be.

Chapter 12: Eating Disorders

Julia was a fourteen-year-old girl. In many ways, she was just like the other girls in her eighth-grade class at Roosevelt Middle School. She did well in some subjects—algebra and Spanish were standouts—but not so well in others. On the girls' soccer team, she played defense. She liked to draw and paint, with her favorite subjects being landscapes populated by horses. Her bedroom walls were decorated with posters of pop stars and reality TV show celebrities.

Her mom loved her daughter and would do anything to keep her safe and healthy. But when school started, Yvonne became concerned about Julia's health.

As the weeks passed, Yvonne noticed Julia lost weight. Even on warm days, her daughter dressed in layers. At the breakfast and dinner table, she was preoccupied with her weight, the food she ate, and how many calories were in each item that she picked at. Despite her slender build, she made frequent comments about feeling "fat" or overweight.

One night at dinner—spaghetti and meatballs with a salad—Yvonne noticed Julia carefully selected just a few bits of plain pasta and chewed them for several minutes. Without thinking, Yvonne snapped, "Child, you need to eat the food put in front of you! Those are perfectly good meatballs. You're not leaving this table until you finish your dinner!"

Julia's eyes flamed in anger. "I don't *feel* well!" she retorted, putting down her fork and glaring at her mother.

"Well then, you need to see the *doctor*."

"I'm not going to any doctor! Why are you torturing me?" Julia got up from the table and stormed into the bathroom.

Yvonne followed her and knocked on the door. "Open this door, young lady!" After a few minutes, the door opened and Julia came out. "I'm going to my room," she announced.

Yvonne thought to herself, I don't want to get into a big fight with her tonight. Maybe she'll feel better tomorrow.

Tomorrow came and went, and the conflicts continued. Much to Yvonne's dismay, their life became a series of battles over food and eating. She felt helpless to change her daughter's behavior and get her "back on track." To be sure, Julia had her ups and downs. Some days she was relatively cheerful and seemed to enjoy eating the tiny portions of bland food Yvonne was now serving her. At other times, she was adamant that she had a weight problem and couldn't possibly eat another fat-filled bite. She refused to eat certain foods and announced she was never going to eat any animal products again, including eggs and milk. While she insisted she needed to eat this way, she also complained of abdominal pain, feeling cold, and constant tiredness. On the soccer team, her coach put her on second string because she wasn't playing well. This was despite her new infatuation with exercise, which, she told her mother, was necessary to avoid getting fat.

Yvonne decided to call the school nurse. They talked for a while in the nurse's office while Julia was in class. The nurse knew Julia and told Yvonne that her daughter might have had anorexia nervosa, an eating disorder characterized by abnormally low body weight, an intense fear of gaining weight, and a distorted perception of weight.

"How could she get such a terrible disease?" said Yvonne. "It must be my fault. I've tried so hard to be a good mother, but you know how it is, with the divorce and work and all the things that happen in life."

"Therapy can help," said the nurse. She gave Yvonne a phone number. "You were smart to come to me soon after noticing the symptoms. The sooner we get Julia into treatment, the better the odds for a full recovery."

"You can recover?" said Yvonne. "The only thing I know about anorexia is the famous singer—Karen Carpenter. She died from it, didn't she?"

"She did, but she had it for many years," replied the nurse. "With affirmative action taken early, Julia has a very good chance to return to a normal healthy life."

Psychological Diseases That Affect Children

Every day, parents from all walks of life receive the unsettling news that their son or daughter is showing signs of any one of several behavioral disorders that lead to self-harm. These may include:

Obsessive-Compulsive Disorder (OCD)

Characterized by obsessions (recurrent, persistent, unwanted, and intrusive thoughts, urges, or images) followed by compulsions (repetitive behaviors or mental acts that patients feel driven to do) to try to lessen or prevent the anxiety that obsessions cause. It can encompass:

Body-focused repetitive behavior disorder, which is characterized by behaviors such as nail-biting, lip biting, cheek chewing.

Body dysmorphic disorder, characterized by an obsession with perceived defects in physical appearance that are not apparent to other people.

Trichotillomania, characterized by recurrent pulling out of one's hair (eyebrows, body hair, hair on the head), resulting in hair loss.

Excoriation disorder, characterized by recurrent picking of one's skin, resulting in skin lesions.

Eating Disorders

These involve a persistent disturbance of eating, or of behavior related to eating, that significantly impairs physical health and/or psychosocial functioning. They can include:

Anorexia nervosa, characterized by a morbid fear of obesity, a distorted body image, and a drastic reduction of eating, leading to significantly low body weight.

Bulimia nervosa, characterized by recurrent episodes of binge eating followed by some form of inappropriate compensatory behavior such as purging (self-induced vomiting, laxative or diuretic abuse), fasting, or driven exercise.

Binge eating disorder, which involves repeated episodes of consuming large amounts of food with a feeling of loss of control. Unlike bulimia, it is not followed by inappropriate compensatory behavior, such as self-induced vomiting.

Pica, which is the persistent eating of nonnutritive, nonfood material when it is developmentally inappropriate. The material may include chalk, paper, gum, clay, soap, cloth, hair, string, wool, pebbles, soil, talcum powder, starch, paint, metal, ice, ash, or charcoal.

Nonsuicidal Self-Injury (NSSI)

This is any self-inflicted act causing pain or superficial damage but not intended to cause death. Typical behaviors include burning the skin, typically with a cigarette, or cutting or stabbing the skin with a sharp object such as a razor.

There are many more diseases, both mental and physical, that can affect a child of any age. This book is not intended to provide insight into all of them, or even most of them. If your child shows any symptoms of disease or complains of discomfort of any type, take your child to his or her pediatrician or family doctor.

What's important is how *you*, the affirmative parent, respond to your child developing one of these conditions. As we saw in the story of Yvonne and Julia, Yvonne initially responded the way many parents would—with a knee-jerk reaction and a demand that the child changes her behavior. In this case, she wanted Julia to stop complaining and eat her dinner. Fortunately, after an argument, Yvonne realized that her daughter had a serious problem that needed professional attention.

Here's something that many parents have a hard time accepting: Often, kids engage in these harmful behaviors because it makes them *feel better for a moment*. Ask any kid with trichotillomania what it feels like to pluck out a hair, and she's likely to say it feels really good. It's a sensation of tremendous relief. The feeling is fleeting, and then the anxiety begins to build again. But for a brief moment, the child was in *control* and *focused*, and because the effect was pleasing, she'll do it again.

The Affirmative Parenting Response

How you respond to anorexia is a good example of how you should respond to any such psychological condition that does not require hospitalization. Here are the steps to take:

1. Watch, Ask, and Listen

When you first see signs of an eating disorder, or any other condition, unless you believe your child is in imminent danger of harm or death, take a deep breath and stay calm. Chances are good that if you're seeing it now, your child has been secretly doing it for a while. It's a part of his or her life.

At a quiet time, with no pressure, sit down with your child and gently ask them about how they feel about eating. Allow them to make their case as to why they need to do what they're doing. Remember, as a parent your first job is to *gather information*. It's in your child's best interest that he or she can confide in you, even if your child blames you. ("It sucks that we had to move to this horrible neighborhood," etc.)

When asked directly, your child is likely to deny there is a problem. It's common for children with eating disorders to not even be aware they have a problem. This is called anosognosia.

Don't insist there is a problem. Be calm and observe him or her closely. Take it step by step.

2. Do Not Blame Yourself

A common parental response to learning their child has any problem or illness is to blame themselves, or worse yet, blame the *other* parent. Don't! What matters now is that you think about the future, and work with your child to bring him or her back to a healthy lifestyle. Your child needs you to be strong; neither wishing the problem would go away nor demanding your child make herself better will produce good results. Never forget that your goal is to help your child to become an adult who is happy, loving, self-sufficient, and engaged in life. To do that requires patience, faith, and objectivity.

3. Get Informed

Start learning about your child's condition. Go online, read books, and talk to healthcare professionals. Don't talk to people who cannot be trusted to act with discretion, or who will dispense uninformed nonsense.

Getting to the truth can be difficult. The causes of diseases like anorexia nervosa can be very complex, and there are many unproven and baseless theories about its roots. Some of the supposed causes include our culture that glorifies thinness (although our culture is changing, and nowadays kids see many body types in the media); women's fashion magazines aimed at teenaged and twenty-something readers; and the highly profitable weight loss industry that constantly preaches the virtues of losing weight.

The truth is that millions of young people, especially girls, are steeped in this culture and don't become anorexic.

Some experts assert family dysfunction lies at the core of anorexia, and it may play a part. As a parent, you need to set aside feelings of guilt, because they are useless; but you also need to be willing to take an objective look at your home life and see if it can be causing unusually high levels of stress in your child. As we know from adverse childhood experiences, chronic or sharp stress can permanently alter the hormone balance in a child, leading to changes in behavior.

Genetics may also be a factor. Some eating disorders are known to be prevalent in certain families, and disorders can appear in twins, as they share the same genes. But the source is not so much in the patient's DNA as it is in her gene expression, which is how the DNA instructions are translated into real-life cellular functions. Changes in the genetic expression are not always bad; they can go either toward disease or better health. Good nutrition is a factor. It can prevent the expression of the genes for anorexia and restore physical health to patients already suffering from the disease.

Hormones can influence gene expression and therefore behavior. Some adult women experience eating disorders that come and go with their menstrual cycle.

Research has suggested that anorexia produces a vicious circle of responses in which the state of starvation can itself produce the symptoms of anorexia, which means that as the disease progresses it *reinforces itself* by changing the brain's chemistry. In 1944, the Minnesota Starvation Experiment tested the effects of food deprivation on volunteer men. For 24 weeks they consumed a restricted diet of 1,600 calories per day while remaining physically active. The lack of food produced not only the expected extreme weight loss but also pronounced psychological effects: depression, obsessive-compulsive behavior (mostly rituals involving food), anxiety, irritability, and delusional thinking. The family and social connections of the volunteers began to disintegrate, their ability to concentrate was impaired, and their comprehension and judgment became sub-optimal.

Even after the men's caloric intake was restored, they continued to suffer psychological effects, with many experiencing severe depression and distress. The researchers dubbed this "semi-starvation neurosis."

The Minnesota Starvation Experiment clearly showed that eating too little food for a prolonged time causes psychological symptoms similar to those of patients with anorexia nervosa. At the outset, the volunteers were tested and found to be psychologically healthy. Their psychological symptoms didn't cause anorexia. The opposite occurred: the symptoms emerged as a consequence of starvation.

This means that if your child has been practicing anorexia for some time, they are likely to be suffering from nutritional deficiencies that can alter the way they think.

4. Visit Your Pediatrician

Make an appointment with your child's pediatrician. The pediatrician or family doctor is the first stop for a general consult, physical exam, and blood tests. It's also probably required by your healthcare plan, because your doctor, who is likely not a specialist, will need to issue a referral.

You're probably already wondering about the cost. Most insurance plans cover specific medical treatments, including nutritional support, and plans may also cover counseling services. But the coverage limits can vary dramatically from one plan to another. Contact your insurer to find out what they cover.

Remember to be non-judgmental. Don't tell your child she's being sent to the doctor to "fix her problem." Tell her you want her to feel better and be happy, and it's going to be okay. Hopefully, your child will trust you enough to go along. If your child refuses to listen to you, talk to a school guidance counselor or school nurse.

From this initial visit you want to get a picture of your child's overall health, especially his or her nutritional status.

5. Find an Eating Disorders Specialist

Ask your pediatrician for referrals to eating disorder specialists in your area. Reputable sites to find treatment providers include:

The Alliance for Eating Disorders Awareness
The National Eating Disorders Association

The Academy for Eating Disorders

The Training Institute for Child and Adolescent Eating Disorders

Familiarize yourself with the different types of treatment.

Psychotherapy has long been the first line of treatment for anorexia, followed by prescription drugs.

Cognitive behavioral therapy (CBT) centers around identifying distorted thinking behaviors, challenging them, and replacing them with rational beliefs.

Dialectical behavior therapy (DBT) emphasizes the acceptance and validation of the patient as a means of helping her to change.

None of these three approaches targets the existing nutritional deficiencies that create the vicious cycle of anorexia, leading to depression from malnutrition, and then to more anorexia.

Family therapy works primarily with the patient and her family. The Maudsley model centers around the family exerting continuous pressure on the child to eat a balanced diet. But many experts fault the "tough love" aspects of this approach and urge a more nuanced approach.

6. Be Careful with Drugs

Unfortunately, we live in a culture in which many well-meaning doctors feel compelled to write a prescription for every disease. When presented with psychological conditions, many highly trained healthcare professionals often prescribe one or more drugs on a "test" basis to "see what happens." Eventually, a patient can be taking multiple psychiatric medications, all with significant side effects.

There are four categories of medications that are often prescribed for patients with anorexia.

Antidepressants can be useful in alleviating the patient's depression and therefore easing the impulse toward anorexia or other self-harming disorders. They work by acting on the neurotransmitters serotonin, norepinephrine, and dopamine.

Antihistamines have produced some results. The antihistamine cyproheptadine has been found to stimulate the appetite and facilitate weight restoration.

Anti-anxiety medications are sometimes prescribed to treat the anxiety and panic associated with mealtime, eating, and weight gain. This is a class of medications called benzodiazepines, including Ativan, Klonopin, Valium, and Xanax.

Antipsychotics are believed to loosen the grip of irrational beliefs, allowing the patient to escape the prison of delusional thinking.

Serotonin Norepinephrine Reuptake Inhibitors (SNRIs) are also used to address comorbid obsessive-compulsive issues but have a relatively neutral effect on weight.

While drugs can be useful, make sure the doctor is prescribing them only as part of a comprehensive program of wellness that includes counseling (perhaps for both parent and child) and proper nutrition. Don't count on a cure being found in a pill bottle.

7. Seek Support for Yourself

Caring for a child with a psychological disorder can be a difficult experience. Many parents benefit from the support and wisdom of other parents who have had a similar experience. Good support resources for parents of children with anorexia include NEDA's Parent, Family & Friends Network (PFN) and the Around the Dinner Table Forum of F.E.A.S.T.

There are also some Facebook groups, including International Eating Disorder Family support.

Remember, early intervention greatly improves prognosis. Affirmative parenting means being *aware* of what your children are doing, *investigating* unusual or harmful behavior, *refraining* from being judgmental, and *guiding* your child with love and compassion back towards wellness.

Chapter 13: Tiger Mom, Elephant Mom, Helicopter Parent

While the title of this chapter suggests a flight to the jungle, it describes a very meaningful debate that's raging among parents and parenting professionals.

The term "tiger mother" (or more colloquially, "tiger mom") was introduced to the world by Yale Law School professor Amy Chua in her 2011 memoir *Battle Hymn of the Tiger Mother*. This largely Chinese-American concept evoked strict parenting styles typically enforced throughout households in East Asia, South Asia, and Southeast Asia.

It's helpful to view the tiger mom concept in its original cultural context. China is a highly stratified society, with little tolerance for original thinkers or nonconformists. The only way to achieve career success in China is to make your way up through the system, which means acquiring socially approved credentials. For children, this means excellence in school and university. For the Chinese, formal education has traditionally been considered the sole means for achieving upward social mobility, and today, national examinations such as the *Gaokao* remain the primary path to career success.

Most Chinese parents—both mothers and fathers—believe that arming children with in-demand job skills such as mathematical and scientific proficiency, strong work habits, and inner confidence is the only way to prepare them for a competitive future. They see the Western approach of "letting the child find his own way" and "encouraging creativity" to be foolish, if not dangerous.

The tiger mom philosophy is driven by a relentless pragmatism: If something does not support the child's chances of getting into a top university, then it has no value.

Classical violin lessons are an asset. Playing folk guitar is a waste of time.

Learning how to write a business report is an asset. Writing a novel is a waste of time.

There is an emotional price to pay for the relentless drive to academic success. If the child strays from the path, he or she is bluntly informed they are worthless and are a disgrace to the family. In Chua's memoir, she relates an incident when she yelled at her daughters, calling them "garbage" in public. Many tiger parents do not allow their children to make personal decisions on their own, whether in daily life or at school. For instance, Chua's daughters were not allowed to watch TV at night or have sleepovers with their schoolmates, because these worthless activities did not contribute to success.

Make no mistake—there are tiger dads, too. You see them most often on the sidelines of school sporting events—hockey, soccer, football. They're the ones yelling at the referee, yelling at the coach, yelling at their own child. They live vicariously through their children, and if the child isn't a champion on the field, the father has been disgraced. Talk about pressure!

In contrast, the term "elephant mom" was introduced in a 2014 article by Priyanka Sharma-Sindhar in *The Atlantic*, to describe her *laissez-faire* upbringing. Rather than demanding strict guidelines that must be followed, elephant moms (or dads) allow their children flexibility and choices. They encourage them to be whoever they want to be and don't force them to conform to a predetermined program aimed at conventional success. To the elephant mom, her child's penchant for folk guitar is every bit as worthy as classical violin, and she would be thrilled if her child announced she was starting to write a novel.

Assuming that both types of parents sincerely want their children to succeed in life, what accounts for the difference in philosophies?

It's simple: The tiger mom believes she knows what will be necessary for success in the future—that is, ten or twenty years from now. She prepares her child for the future based on what she sees in the world today, and on the most obvious paths to self-reliance: doctor, lawyer, business manager. What is unseen has no value. And the opinion of the child, who does not have the life experience of the adult, is irrelevant.

The elephant mom does *not know* what will be necessary for success in the future. She believes the world is big and constantly changing, and you can't tell what avenues for success will be waiting for a child. People can be successful in doing all sorts of things, including working in industries that may not yet exist. When I was growing up, there was no solar panel industry. A kid at school who was interested in solar energy would have been regarded as someone with an interesting hobby. While a tiger mom would have strongly discouraged an interest in solar energy because there was no future in it, an elephant mom would say, "You love solar energy? Go for it."

There is a third category of parent: the helicopter parent. The term was first used in Dr. Haim Ginott's 1969 book *Parents & Teenagers* by teens who said their parents would hover over them like a helicopter; by 2011 the term became popular enough to become a dictionary entry. Similar terms include "lawnmower parenting," "cosseting parent," or "bulldoze parenting."

These people hover over their children, removing obstacles, clearing the path for success. They ply their trade at every age. "In toddlerhood," psychologist Ann Dunnewold, Ph.D., told Parents.com, "a helicopter parent might constantly shadow the child, always playing with and directing his behavior, allowing him zero alone time." This extends into school age, with the helicopter parent arranging for the child to have a particular teacher or coach, choosing the child's friends and activities, or providing heavy-handed assistance for homework and school projects.

The critical difference between a tiger mom and a helicopter parent is that the former believes her child is inherently flawed and must be made better, while the latter believes her child is inherently perfect and must be protected from corrupting influences.

As I write this, a flagrant case of helicopter parenting is in the news: the 2019 college admissions bribery scandal, in which thirty-three parents of college applicants are accused of paying more than $25 million between 2011 and 2018 to the organizer of the scheme, who in turn used the money to fraudulently inflate the students' entrance exam test scores and bribe college officials. Numerous schemes were used to game the system, including fraudulently claiming the student had a learning disability, which qualified him or her for extra time taking the SAT or ACT test. Students were falsely portrayed as being varsity athletes, and even photos were faked showing the student competing. College coaches were bribed to attest to the fact that the student was a recruit for the college team.

Felicity Huffman, who pled guilty to one count of conspiracy to commit mail fraud and honest services mail fraud, stemming from a payment of $15,000 she made to facilitate cheating for her daughter on the SATs, said in court:

"My daughter knew absolutely nothing about my actions, and in my misguided and profoundly wrong way, I have betrayed her.

This transgression toward her and the public I will carry for the rest of my life. My desire to help my daughter is no excuse to break the law or engage in dishonesty."

The Four Parenting Styles

Popular culture aside, psychologists have identified four basic parenting styles. This system is based on the work of Diana Baumrind, a developmental psychologist at the University of California at Berkeley. In the 1960s, she noticed that the behavior of preschoolers was highly correlated to a specific kind of parenting. Her theory was that there was a close relationship between the child-raising styles of parents and their children's behavior, which she observed in preschool.

Baumrind initially identified three different parenting styles: authoritative parenting, authoritarian parenting, and permissive parenting. In 1983, researchers E.E. Maccoby and J.A. Martin expanded this parenting style model to include a fourth, neglectful parenting.

1. Authoritarian

The tiger mom is a type of authoritarian parent. They believe parents make the rules and kids should follow them without exception. When a child questions the reasons behind a rule, the authoritarian parent will reply, "Because I said so." They are not interested in negotiating and their focus is on obedience. The opinion of the child is of no importance, and can even be dangerous. These parents use ironclad discipline and often employ punishment to control children's behavior.

Baumrind found that children of authoritarian parents often have an unhappy disposition, are less independent, appear insecure, and possess lower self-esteem. In short, they can't think or act autonomously.

2. Authoritative

The elephant mom is a type of authoritative parent. They have high expectations for achievement and maturity, but this is supported by emotional warmth and responsiveness. They set rules and enforce boundaries not by decree but by using reasoning and having an open discussion. They encourage independence and use positive discipline strategies to reinforce good behavior, such as praise and reward systems.

Children of authoritative parents are likely to appear happy and content, be independent, achieve higher academic success, exhibit good self-esteem, and are able to interact with peers using competent social skills.

3. Permissive

The helicopter parent falls into this category. These parents are warm and loving but set very few rules and boundaries, and they are reluctant to enforce limits. They may be totally *laissez-faire* and let the child roam at will, or, like helicopter parents, continually intervene to smooth the way for the child.

Permissive parents are more comfortable playing the role of their child's friend rather than a parent. They fear to lose the affection of their child, even temporarily. While they encourage their children to talk with them about their problems, they refuse to judge and don't put much effort into limiting bad behavior or discouraging poor choices.

While they may be emotionally close to their parents, children of permissive parents have difficulty following rules, show poor self-control, and have more problems in relationships and social interactions. Because permissive parents are unwilling to limit junk food intake, their children may be at a higher risk for health problems such as obesity. Because their parents ensured they always got what they wanted, they may exhibit a sense of entitlement.

4. Neglectful

Neglectful or uninvolved parents expect children to raise themselves. They don't, or can't, devote much time or energy to meeting their children's basic needs. They do not set firm boundaries or high standards, and are uninvolved in their children's lives.

There are two categories of neglectful parents: those who are neglectful through no intention of their own, such as those with mental health issues, substance abuse problems, or job issues; and those who are perfectly capable of managing a household but simply choose not to. The latter types are often those who feel pressure to excel at work and use that as an excuse to avoid family responsibilities.

Absent parents are more likely to have mental issues themselves, such as maternal depression, child neglect, physical abuse, stemming from when they were kids.

Children of neglectful parents feel fundamentally unloved. They tend to be dismissive of authority, are more impulsive, cannot regulate their emotions, experience more addiction, and delinquency problems, and suffer from more mental issues, such as suicidal behavior. They're more likely to view the world as a dog-eat-dog environment where only the strong survive.

The Affirmative Parent

What's the right course for the affirmative parent? It's simple:

1. Encourage your child to try new things.

2. Support them in what *they're* interested in.

3. Provide a safe and secure "home base" to which they can always return.

4. Impress upon them the importance of *taking care of the basics*: getting good grades, getting a job, being self-sufficient.

5. Lead by example. Show your child the type of adult you want them to become.

Remember the goal: You want your child to become an adult who is happy, loving, self-sufficient, and engaged in life. One of the keywords is "self-sufficient." This means letting your child make mistakes and offering a helping hand to lift them to their feet and try again.

Chapter 14: The Truth About the Child's Biological Parent

This is the last chapter in the book because it tackles a question that is fundamental to your child's sense of identity: "Who am I?"

In our culture, the number of families with two biological parents—a mother and a father—is declining. I'm not going to comment on why this is so, or what it means; that's something I will leave to others. My job is to equip you and your child-raising partner (if you have one) with the tools to help your child grow up to become an adult who is happy, loving, self-sufficient, and engaged in life.

Imagine—if you have not already lived through this—a baby whose father has died. Infants have little awareness of what's *supposed* to be; they only know what *is*. If the big person taking care of them happens to be a woman or two women, then the infant, who knows nothing about life on the strange planet, and who has no frame of reference, will accept this as normal.

Likewise, if the parents are black and the baby is white, or if there's no female in the house, only two men. The infant will accept these conditions as normal.

But eventually, when the child grows older and develops a sense of not only self-awareness but an awareness of what other families are like, they may start to wonder, "Why am I different?"

Another common scenario is when you start to realize that while the child's adoptive parents have been a wonderful and nurturing presence, every human being deserves to know who their biological parents are, even if the missing biological parent is incarcerated or living on Skid Row.

The issue is exceedingly complex.

Consider the article that novelist Lisa Lutz wrote in 2012 for *The New York Times*. Entitled "I Found My Biological Parents, and Wish I Hadn't," she related how she was never very close to her adoptive parents. "I didn't feel a strong bond with the parents who raised me," she wrote, "and I had anything but a happy childhood.... I felt as if I were living with complete strangers." She knew she was adopted, and the knowledge "untethered me from some of that unhappiness. I was alone but happily so. I was free to make up any story I wanted about where I came from."

When she was twenty-five, she had a phone conversation with her birth mother. They then exchanged letters, and that was it. Neither mother nor daughter wanted to pursue the relationship.

At the age of thirty-seven, she met "biodad," as she called him. The event was underwhelming. She journeyed to a town in central California, and he picked her up in his windowless Jeep and drove her to a mobile home park, where she met her biological uncle and grandmother. After spending the afternoon chatting, she left, and that was the end of it. She wrote, "When I finally had time to take it all in, I felt like the result of a mishandled science experiment." She met both her biological parents and accepted the fact that while they both may have been law-abiding people, they were lousy parents, and felt none of that special parent-child bond.

Other adopted children have amazing tales to tell. The film *Three Identical Strangers* tells the story of Robert Shafran, David Kellman, and Eddy Galland, three identical triplets who were separated at birth and given to the Louise Wise Adoption Agency in New York City. Each baby was adopted by a different family, and as they grew up, they were never told of the existence of the others. When they finally met at age nineteen, they—and the public—were astounded at how much alike they were.

But why were they separated and the adoptions kept a secret?

It turned out that the triplets were part of a secret study in which newborn identical siblings who had been put up for adoption were separated for the purpose of psychological and behavioral experimentation. The study was supposed to determine how much of a person's behavior is hereditary and how much is shaped by their environment (nature vs. nurture), using identical siblings raised in different households as the control group.

The brothers were not happy to discover they had been used like lab rats; when he learned the truth, Robert Shafran said, "This is, like, Nazi s--t."

To get back to your situation, the big question is, "When do I tell my child the truth about his or her parent? And how much should I tell?"

As difficult as it is, the answer is this: No one—no expert, no child psychologist—knows when or how much your child should be told. You will have to decide that for yourself.

All you can know for sure is that your child will eventually learn the truth. That is a *certainty*. The only remaining question is when, and under what circumstances.

While you think about it, here are some factors to consider.

If possible, tell the child when they are young, so that they grow up knowing the truth. This helps the knowledge to be less dramatic and simply a part of life.

Don't invent silly stories. Just tell the truth. If young children hear terms like "stepfamily" and "stepparent" used positively and openly from the start, a relaxed atmosphere will be created around the subject long before they fully understand what the words mean.

Tell your child that all families are different, and remind him or her about all the people who love them.

You need to think about who else needs to know. While there's no need to broadcast the family business to the world, people who come into contact with your child should know, because you don't want them blurting out something thoughtless.

Along the same lines, avoid asking your child to keep this information secret, as this may cause him or her to feel guilty and ashamed.

If a parent has passed away, be open and honest. Encourage the child to express their emotions, and help them cope with their grief as best you can. If you follow a certain religion, you'll probably couch the explanation in those terms, which you have every right to do. Don't say, "Daddy has gone to sleep forever," because it isn't true and will give your child a horrible idea about sleep.

Above all, no matter what the reason for the absence of the biological parent, be sure to make it clear that it is *not the fault of the child*. If you don't assure them otherwise, a child of any age may feel as though they are responsible for the absence, or will feel guilty because they think they could have done something more to keep mommy or daddy around.

If the child's parent is incarcerated, I encourage you to go online and seek a support group. Many of them are religion-based, so you'll have to shop around to find one that matches your belief system. The important thing to remember is that children have an uncanny way of learning the truth. Most families find that when they make well-meaning attempts to try to conceal the fact that a family member is in prison, children always figure out the truth. It's even worse when a child finds out from a cruel classmate that his or her parent is actually incarcerated rather than being "away" or "living in another town." As soon as you feel able to deal with the matter truthfully, it's always better to be honest with your children. While the immediate impact may hurt them and cause them to become angry, it's usually best to give children as long as possible to adjust to the reality of their life.

You have to judge for yourself what you tell a child about an absentee parent. Some social workers advise partners of absent parents to say to the child, "Daddy (or mommy) loves you very much, but just can't be with you for a while." This sounds nice, but then the child will eventually think, "Well, if daddy loves me so much, how come he's never here?" It's a lose-lose situation. The best thing you can do for your child is to be as honest as possible and then say, "But remember, I love you, and there are many people who love you, and we want you to grow up to be happy, loving, self-sufficient, and engaged in life. And that's what you deserve!"

It's what every child deserves.

Thank You

Thank you for reading this book. I welcome your comments and shared wisdom. I invite you to contact me:

    dalessheffieldphd@gmail.com
    www.drdalesheffield.com

About the Author

Dr. Sheffield graduated from North Carolina State University with a Ph.D. in Counselor Education in May 1999 and opened his private practice a few weeks later in Raleigh, NC. He is a Licensed Clinical Mental Health Counselor Supervisor, a Licensed Clinical Mental Health Counselor, and a National Certified Counselor. He works with adults, adolescents, children, parents, couples, and families.

Before receiving his Ph.D., he earned a Master's Degree in Counselor Education with a focus in agency counseling from The University of North Carolina at Greensboro, graduating in May 1992. From July 1992 until August 1996, he worked for a family service agency and two different county mental health centers in North Carolina before moving to Raleigh to pursue his doctoral studies.

Dr. Sheffield is a member of the American Counseling Association, the American Mental Health Counselors Association, and the Licensed Professional Counselors Association of North Carolina. He is a lifetime member of the Chi Sigma Iota Counseling and Professional Honor Society.

Publications

Sheffield, D.S., Baker, S. (2005). Themes from retrospective interviews of school counselors who experienced burnout. Hacettepe Universitesi Journal of Education, 29, 177-186.

Sheffield, D. S. (1998). Counselor impairment: Moving toward a concise definition and protocol. Journal of Humanistic Counseling, 37(2), 96-106.

Jones, L. K., Sheffield, D., Joyner, B. (2000). Comparing the effects of the Career Key with the Self-Directed Search and the Job-OE among eighth-grade students. Professional School Counseling, 3(4), 238-247.

Acknowledgements

I want to thank my wife for her enthusiasm and support throughout this process; and my daughter, Annie Sheffield, for her help producing and distributing this book.

I also want to thank Thomas Hauck for his breadth of knowledge and sage advice regarding self-help books; Maryanne Livingston from HIGH PERFORMANCE MARKETING. INC. for her creativity and artistic skills in designing a beautiful front and back cover for the book; Candia Rasmussen from Lundie's Photography for her professionalism and artistic abilities; and Benjamin Bertolini for his professionalism and persistence in capturing the essence of our family.

Made in United States
Orlando, FL
09 April 2025